THE AMERICAN STAGE OF TO-DAY

BIOGRAPHIES
AND PHOTOGRAPHS
OF
ONE HUNDRED
LEADING
ACTORS AND
ACTRESSES
WITH
AN INTRODUCTION BY
WILLIAM WINTER

NEW YORK
P F COLLIER & SON
MCMX

350036

Copyright, 1909, by P. F. Collier & Son

THE AMERICAN STAGE OF TO-DAY

A LIST OF THE PLAYERS

Maude Adams
Viola Allen
Margaret Anglin
Macklyn Arbuckle
George Arliss
Ethel Barrymore
John Barrymore
Blanche Bates
Kyrle Bellew
Edmund Breese
Billie Burke
Marie Cahill
Mrs. Carter
Marguerite Clarke
Gertrude Coghlan
Rose Coghlan
George M. Cohan
William Collier
Ida Conquest
W. H. Crane
Henrietta Crosman
Arnold Daly
Frank Daniels
Henry E. Dixey
J. E. Dodson

Marie Doro
John Drew
Robert Edeson
Maxine Elliott
Grace Ellison
Douglas Fairbanks
William Faversham
Elsie Ferguson
Lew Fields
Grace Filkins
Mrs. Fiske
Bertha Galland
Adeline Genée
Grace George
William Gillette
Lulu Glaser
N. C. Goodwin
James K. Hackett
Virginia Harned
Anna Held
Crystal Herne
Raymond Hitchcock
William Hodge
E. M. Holland
De Wolf Hopper

A LIST OF THE PLAYERS

Isabel Irving
May Irwin
Louis James
Elsie Janis
Bertha Kalish
Doris Keane
Frank Keenan
Herbert Kelcey
Wilton Lackaye
Cecilia Loftus
Louis Mann
Mary Mannering
Robert Mantell
Julia Marlowe
John Mason
Henry Miller
Tim Murphy
Alla Nazimova
Carlotta Neilson
Olga Nethersole
William Norris
Chauncey Olcott
James O'Neill
Nance O'Neill
Julie Opp

James T. Powers
Ada Rehan
Hedwig Reicher
Charles Richman
Annie Russell
Lillian Russell
Florence Roberts
Eleanor Robson
May Robson
Julia Sanderson
Fritzi Scheff
Effie Shannon
Otis Skinner
E. H. Sothern
Ruth St. Denis
Rose Stahl
Frances Starr
Mabel Taliaferro
Charlotte Walker
Blanche Walsh
David Warfield
Walker Whiteside
Hattie Williams
Francis Wilson
Olive Wyndham

FOREWORD

By WILLIAM WINTER

"Let them be well used, for they are the abstract and brief chronicles of the time"

IT IS a self-evident proposition that, primarily and naturally, the general public is less interested in the Theatre of the Past and in the Theatre of the Future than it is in the Theatre of the Present. *Laudator temporis acti* is considered a bore and is designated "a back number." The prophet is viewed as a dreamer and is dismissed as a fool. "The present eye," says Shakespeare, "praises the present object." Yet, probably, it would not be denied, even by the most ardent enthusiast of the Present, that the possession of ample, exact, and particular knowledge of the Theatre of Yesterday is essential to persons whose vocation is the management of the Theatre of To-day. Theatrical history, therefore, it can be reasoned, possesses a practical value, and, because of its practical value, ought to be fully and accurately written. Students of the Theatre of the distant Past are, meanwhile, aware that the chronicles of it, while large in quantity, and various in form, are diffuse in method, often contradictory, widely scattered, silent as to some important matters, and vexatiously indefinite as to others; and, furthermore, that those chronicles are, for the most part, secluded from the reach of all persons except antiquarians, in files of old periodicals, or on the dim and dusty shelves of more or less inaccessible libraries. Such students also know that those chronicles, when discovered and explored, are often found to be unsatisfactory, because of their lack of minute, specific information, and also because of their ill-digested opinion. Various adjectives could be found, relative to Burbage, Betterton, Elizabeth Barry, Barton Booth, Anne Oldfield, Garrick, Peg Woffington, Kemble, and Mrs. Siddons; but, after long and careful investigation, the most discriminative of analytical thinkers would find it impossible to ascertain in exactly what manner Betterton acted *Hamlet* or Garrick acted *King Lear*, or by what means Anne Oldfield fascinated with *Lady Townly*, or Mrs. Siddons broke the public heart with *Mrs. Beverley* or *Jane Shore*. It is not until the student endeavors to find a complete, verbal picture, a clear, detailed statement, or a definite, positive conclusion, in those old theatrical chronicles (such as Downes, Langbaine, Chetwood, Victor, Genest, and even Dunlap), that he begins to realize how bewildering and frustrating they often are and what a blessing it would be if theatrical history had always been written with continuity of luminous narrative, amplitude of precise detail, and exactitude of specification. In the present period of comprehensive journalism much more scrupulous attention is given to the proceedings of actors than was ever given before (though it should be noted that there are useful biographies of a few actors conspicuous in the nineteenth century), and the printed record of those proceedings is not less particular than voluminous. It becomes possible, accordingly, for the historian of the contemporary drama, if he chooses to compel himself to minute observation and exact statement, to portray the precise personality of cotaneous actors, define their several styles, and depict the rationale of the performances by which they have obtained renown.

It is essential to consider that the Theatre is not a building or an aggregate of buildings in which theatrical performances are given, but a social institution, like Literature, or any other form of Art. The

FOREWORD

natural phrase, so much in common use, "our Theatre," possesses a very positive significance. A feeling exists toward the Theatre, and has long existed, entirely unlike the feeling entertained toward shops and commodities. The People regard the Theatre as a part of their mental patrimony; as a rightful possession; as something to which they are *entitled* and in which they are intimately and seriously concerned. Readers of the history of Drury Lane, in London, and of the Old Park, in New York, find that feeling manifested with peculiar ardor. In recent years and in American cities, on the other hand, the proclaimed standard of theatrical administration is that which treats the Theatre as on a level with the mart of hides, tallow, pickles, and "notions." Yet, strangely enough, it has been judicially decided, in the State of New York, that admission to a dramatic performance,—essentially a matter of barter between manager and public,—is *not* a commodity, and that the huckster who vends it may sell it to one and withhold it from another, at his caprice, and that after it has been sold, that huckster can, if he likes, prevent the purchaser making use of it, by debarring him from the theatre: in short, that the Theatre is a personal, private affair, in which the People have no rights. That is not the view taken by the community at large, and never has been,—for the decisive reason that the Theatre enters into the every-day life and bears directly upon the mental and moral condition of the public, and especially upon the morals and lives of the young. The right view of our Theatre is that which accounts it an asset of civilization, and, as such, protects and fosters it, keeping pure the spirit and keeping high the intellectual standard of all that it displays. The essential matter is the vital principle, not the environment. The buildings which, in this period, are provided for theatrical representations are far more commodious than those which were provided for such purposes in former times, but the welfare and advancement of the Theatre do not mainly consist in the bettering of its habitation, and cannot be measured by a standard of mere physical investiture: as remarked by *Don Pedro:* "The vizor is Philemon's roof,—within the house is Jove." The life of the Theatre has always consisted, and always will consist, in the development of the Art of Acting and in maintenance of perfect public sympathy with that art, and these are matters in which the tradesman is not involved, and to which that much besought "regeneration of the Drama," so frequently mentioned, of late years, as the sovereign panacea for all theatrical ills, could not in any way contribute. Good new plays, of course, are desirable. There could not be too many of them. But we do not lack "representative drama." Both here and abroad there are as many plays representative of current phases of actual life as there have been in any former period, and it would be foolish to disparage good plays, rep-

EDWIN BOOTH
AS
HAMLET

resentative of any period, from any source, upon any stage, and, most of all, on the stage of an heterogeneous population, in process of being blended into one people. The imperative need of our Theatre,—and it *is* imperative,—is, not more plays, but better Acting. The relation of plays to Acting is analogous to the relation of colors to painting. Without colors there could be no painting: without plays there could be no acting: but the loveliest of colors are useless,

FOREWORD

except for the genius and skill of the artist who knows how to employ them, and the finest of plays,—although, of course, they could be read,—must fall far short of their purpose, except for the genius and skill of the actors, to give them form, voice, light, and feeling, making them evident for the vision and the hearing, and sending them home to the public heart.

LAWRENCE BARRETT
AS
CASSIUS

The corner-stone of the whole fabric of the Theatre, accordingly, is the Actor. In him is vested the intellectual faculty to guide genial emotion, and it is by genial emotion that the human race is led. His vocation, therefore, is of great public importance, and a solemn responsibility rests upon him to pursue it with a deep conviction and clear sense of duty—to allow no subjects on the stage that will defile the minds of his auditors, and to liberate and stimulate only those feelings by which human nature is ennobled. Thus McCullough did, when he acted *Virginius;* no listener that ever heard his voice, in that great Forum scene—"Does no one speak?"—can forget the respondent thrill of emotion that was dispersed through the whole hushed, breathless assemblage. Thus Jefferson did, when, as poor old *Caleb Plummer,* meeting the son supposed to have been drowned at sea, he uttered the hysterical cry, "My boy! my boy! Don't tell me that he is *alive!*" Thus Willard did, as *Cyrus Blenkarn,* when, being told of his idolized daughter's shame and flight, he half whispered to himself, "O, my Mary, my Mary! Why, she was here—only a few minutes ago—and I told her it was better to be dead than to live so. I didn't mean it, my dear, I didn't mean it!" Thus Theodore Roberts did (among living actors a man in the front rank, for ability and achievement), when he appeared in the strange, composite, semi-savage character of *Joe Portugais,* and, in a scene of wonderful pathos, gave such expression to horror, agony and remorse as would be possible only to a nature rich in emotion and an art precisely and perfectly balanced and controlled. Such examples clarify the meaning of what is claimed for the Theatre, and point the way upon which the actor's art should move. If, then, knowledge of the Theatre of the Past is essential to those persons who manage the Theatre of the Present, how much more is it essential to actors, upon whom the very existence of the Theatre depends, and to the Public, whose practical sympathy and interest support them both! Acting, rightly considered, is one of the learned professions,—the Stage being no less important to society than the Pulpit, the Press or the Bar. The more extensive and exact an actor's acquaintance with the styles of acting which have prevailed, in succeeding periods and in various countries,—styles that were sequent upon action and reaction between the Theatre and the People,—the larger and finer will his equipment be, and the more competent and persuasive his procedure, in addressing, and in helping to mold, the taste of the age in which he lives. That great actor Edwin Booth, speaking to the present writer, said: "I like to read about the old dramatists." He could not have chosen a line of reading more illuminative in the study of human nature or more practically helpful in the pursuit of his vocation.

Edwin Booth was one of the representative men, in the great intellectual lineage of Betterton, Garrick, Kemble, Kean, Macready, Cooper, Forrest, and Wallack, who have maintained our Theatre, devel-

FOREWORD

oped the Art of Acting, and brought the stage to the eminence that it holds to-day. His active career ended about twenty years ago and he has been dead since 1893, but his service to the art of acting was so great, his personality was so potential, and his example was so impressive that his influence still subsists, and still is equally an incentive to noble dramatic enterprise and a rebuke to those ignoble dabblers in the Drama who, with their vapid "musical farces," tawdry "leg-shows," and exposures of "Tenderloin" vulgarity and vice, are making it, in as far as they can, a pander to the low appetite of the uncouth mob. One result of Booth's influence, for example, is the erection of the magnificent building, in New York, which has recently been opened, under the designation of The New Theatre. That influence it was which established, and has helped to keep alive, in the minds of thoughtful persons, the deep feeling, the imperative conviction, that the Theatre should be organized on a grand scale. That influence it was which prompted many writers to advocate such a movement. That influence, especially, it was which inflamed the ardent ambition of that brilliant genius and tremendous worker, Richard Mansfield, who desired not only to vie with Edwin Booth but to surpass him, and Mansfield's eloquent appeal to the public spirit and the wealth of this community, for an endowed Theatre, was certainly instrumental in procuring that consummation which now seems possible. Thus it is that a great man's memory survives. Thus it is that the noble work achieved by Edwin Booth has contributed to provide for the people of the great metropolis of America a veritable temple of art, in which it is promised that all things shall be beautiful, and in which, therefore, nothing can be base. When that New Theatre was dedicated, indeed, a distinguished statesman, who addressed the audience, spoke of "the failure of Booth's Theatre." His environment might have admonished him of his error,—for success is not measured by mere monetary gain. The authentic records, had he consulted them, would certainly have done so, for Booth's Theatre, while it *was* Booth's Theatre, was not, in any sense, a failure. That house was opened on February 3, 1869. The auditorium was beautiful in its decorations, but it was not so beautiful as to eclipse the beauty of the stage, and that stage was a marvel of symmetry, appointment, and fitness for the purposes of dramatic representation. Its depth, from the footlights to the rear wall, was fifty-five feet. The arch was seventy-six feet wide. Beneath the stage there was a pit, thirty-two feet deep, which had been dug in the earth and blasted out of the solid rock, into which a whole scene could be sunk, so that it was possible,—as in the splendid production of "Hamlet," which presently ensued,—to save time and to heighten effect by rapidity of scenic change. The flats (for drops, practically, were then unknown), were raised or lowered by pressure from hydraulic rams. Every part of the mechanism of a production of a play could be, and was, constructed within the theatre. The precautions taken against fire were so complete and effectual that the underwriters insured the theatre at rates of from one and a half to two per cent less than was charged for insurance of any other theatre in the city. Booth managed his theatre for

JOSEPH JEFFERSON
AS
RIP VAN WINKLE

FOREWORD

four years, and although it necessitated lavish expense,—more canvas, for example, being required for the setting of a single scene, on Booth's stage, than was required for the setting of a whole five-act comedy on the stage of Wallack's,—the net profit of the

JOHN McCULLOUGH
AS
VIRGINIUS

first season was $102,000; of the second season $85,000; of the third season $70,000. A mortgage of $100,000 was cleared away. The floating debt was reduced from $66,000 to $24,000. Decline in profits was due to the inevitable subsidence of lively popular interest in a new enterprise, but it was never doubtful that, had Booth continued to direct the management of his theatre, its annual profit would have been, at least, $50,000. He retired from management (in June, 1873) because he was weary of it, jaded in mind, by temperament a recluse, and after the panic of that year he went into bankruptcy, under injudicious advice and against his will,—a step, it should particularly be remembered, which was not taken until more than a year after he had ceased to manage Booth's Theatre, and a step which was not, in any way, consequent on his management of that

Theatre, and which it was thought would protect him from extortion. Notwithstanding Booth's lack of business sagacity, his confiding disposition, his indifference to material gain, and his propensity to drift and dream, he earned three successive fortunes, and, dying at the age of sixty, left an estate of more than half a million. His pecuniary success was great, but his greater success was that of mind and soul. He was a great man, and his memory will be honored always in the annals of our stage. Booth's Theatre, after he left it, passed through the custody of various speculative managers, and ultimately it was abandoned: but in his hands it never was a failure, and in endeavors that are now current the spirit of it seems to live again and to breathe a monition to the People to guard and promote the sacred cause of which he made it the emblem: for it is with the People, in their love and enjoyment of acting and in their allegiance to the Actor and his Art, that the Present of the Theatre rests, and it is to the People that its Future is committed.

There is an impression current, to some extent, that the advancement of the Theatre in America is attributable to the "gigantic business enterprise," astute "management," and dexterous financial dealing of persons who, having leased or built many houses, obtained control of many plays, formed a close corporation for their personal benefit and aggrandizement, and "cornered the market," largely dominate the stage; but that is an error—for there is very little of even enlightened self-interest in the theatrical management of this period. It has, indeed, been perceived that the field of the drama is a lucrative one, and susceptible of being made richly responsive to cultivation, and, accordingly, money has been invested in it, and cultivation has been sedulously pursued; but without the Actor, and without a public spirit sympathetic with the Actor, neither "business enterprise," nor shrewdness, nor sharp practice, nor capital could accomplish anything, and recent development in our Theatre, such as it is, has resulted, not from the forces that chiefly control its administration, but in spite of them. It is more than questionable, indeed, whether the condition of the Theatre would not be cleaner and better, its progress swifter, and its influence more salutary, if it were altogether relieved of that "gigantic business enterprise," rescued from the hands of tradesmen, and

FOREWORD

relegated to the control of the Actor, who is the natural and rightful custodian of it.

Facilities for transacting business of every kind, and of theatrical business among the rest, have, of late years, been greatly augmented. In all directions the tendency is toward combination, centralization, organization, and the speculators who have almost entirely absorbed the Theatre of America have been sufficiently susceptible to the trend of the times, and also sufficiently shrewd, to make use of the facilities that combination and organization have supplied. The business of squeezing the orange, accordingly, goes on with vigor and flourishes in rank luxuriance,—although it is conducted with, for example, much the same sagacious and provident forethought which has marked the devastation of the forests of our country,—those speculators having, in fact, done nothing for either the Theatre or the Public. What beneficial influence have they used or even sought to use? What have they done to encourage dramatists of a high order? What provision have they made for the development of actors? What actor has been produced by them? Who are the leading actors of the day? Mantell, Sothern, Mason, Whytal, Kellerd, Worthing, Roberts, Goodwin, Forbes-Robertson, Louis James, Crane, Bellew, Dodson, Cartwright, Tyrone Power, E. M. Holland, James O'Neil, Miss Marlowe, Miss Bates, Miss Allen, Mrs. Fiske,—every one of them was reared in a time when the Actor dominated, and before theatrical "rings," monopolies, or syndicates were regarded. Mantell, for example, had acted many scores of parts before he entered into association with the management under which he now performs: is the excellence of his achievement due to his development, training, and experience, or is it due to "a route in the Syndicate houses"? Miss Blanche Bates, who was recognized as an actress of exceptional talent and auspicious promise long before she entered the service in which she is now employed, has given ten years,— and those her best years,—under the conditions that prevail to-day, and with what result? She has, in all that time, acted *six parts*, only one of which, intrinsically, was worth acting, and she has seen great opportunity slip from her grasp. The only things that can truthfully be claimed for any theatrical "ring" are cynical disregard of all interests except its own, blatant expedition in "doing business," and promptitude in gathering the "rake-off." Nothing fine was ever accomplished by the effort that is prompted by greed of gain. Great works of art proceed from love of art. When acting is made a mere trade, it is degraded, and, at this time, potential influences are more or less effectively operative which, notwithstanding the eminence of the Stage as an institution, tend to make it so. There is great luxury; eager desire to obtain wealth and to obtain it quickly, with little or no regard to integrity of conduct; a fever of unrest; a continuous flurry of haste, and therefore no repose. Means of rapid transportation are ample, over the expanse of a vast country, and, since it has been found that the diffusion of theatrical exhibition is more immediately remunerative than the concentration of it, "star" actors are created, in large numbers and out of poor material,

RICHARD MANSFIELD
AS
KING RICHARD III

FOREWORD

and the inevitable consequence is deterioration in the quality of acting. Rapid and huge increase of population, more or less general access of pecuniary means, and a wide and still widening dissemination of intelligence among the people would, inevitably, augment and intensify demand for theatrical supply, and it

EDWIN FORREST
AS
CORIOLANUS

could not be expected that the demand would be ignored; but that posture of affairs serves only to make more conspicuous the venality of that selfish, reprehensible commercialism which, by mercenary policy and manifold restriction, prevents, at the source, the development of trained actors and the enlargement of the numbers of them, at the very time when such enlargement is most needed. The intellectual obligation to the dramatic art and to the community remains unchanged, and in the minds of some,—perhaps of many,—actors it is ever present, and they would like to fulfil it; but in many cases their training has been inadequate, and in other cases their experience of their surroundings has disheartened, disabled, or corrupted them. There is, for example, no successor to Edwin Booth. Such a style as that of John Gilbert, or William Warren, or John Parselle, or Joseph Jefferson (all representatives of authentic character, as true and as frequent to-day as ever), cannot now anywhere be seen. The rugged, towering personality and the colossal power of Forrest, "four square to opposition," has become a fading memory. The romantic, captivating manliness of Edward L. Davenport, in "St. Marc," and the splendid ardor of Lawrence Barrett, in "The King of the Commons," are forgotten: at all events, nothing of the kind is even suggested, except in the acting of Robert Mantell, and in that of two or three other survivors of the old mode. Our time, undeniably, is one of marvels: especially is it marvellous in science and mechanism: but, unhappily, the spirit of it is, to a considerable extent, unromantic and cynical, and our Theatre partakes of the spirit of our time.

But, notwithstanding materialism, commercialism, and cynicism, human nature remains susceptible to noble and gentle influence, the human heart is responsive to genius and beauty, and the fire of enthusiasm is not wholly extinct, either before the curtain or behind it. While there is much to be deplored in the state of society and in the state of our Theatre, there is also much to be enjoyed and admired. Progress moves in cycles, and portents now visible signify that the old mode is coming round again. Observers, indeed, exist, and are often audible, who scorn it, who think Shakespeare is archaic; that the true road to artistic fruition and social improvement leads through the brothel, the clinic, the cesspool and the charnel-house; that the province of the Theatre is the vivisection of disease and iniquity; that photography is acting; and that tragedians of the Forrest, or Brooke, or Booth, or McCullough, or Barrett, or Vandenhoff school are merely declamatory and elocutionary. Time will answer them, as the veteran Cibber answered the young, colloquial Garrick, when that victorious actor exuberantly exclaimed: "The old style wouldn't do now." "How do you know?" said Cibber; "you never tried it." In its recurrence the old mode will have dispensed with a certain formalism which was obvious in some exponents of it,— even in Mathews and Lester Wallack: if the old actors themselves, such as Davenport, Brooke, Placide, Marshall, Burton, Sefton, Blake, Walcot, Adams, and Owens, were living now, there

MRS. GILBERT
IN
"DOLLARS AND SENSE"

is no reason to doubt that they would, almost involuntarily, adapt their styles to the contemporary preference for complete flexibility of expression: but the old mode will retain its old beauties,—exactitude of sincere impersonation; atmosphere of poetry; precision and clarity of speech; simplicity of action; grace of trained movement; authority of distinction; and an absolute, beguiling sympathy with romance. Jefferson was a typical embodiment of that style, and, to the end of his career, which terminated only about five years ago, he enthralled the public regard, and everywhere found the keenest and amplest appreciation. Ada Rehan, who, in her girlhood, had profited by professional association with that accomplished actress, Mrs. John Drew, and by the example of many veterans with whom it was her fortune to act, had acquired that style, and to the day of her withdrawal from the stage, was so brilliant a type of it that she eclipsed competition in the most difficult comedy character ever written,—Shakespeare's *Rosalind*. Robert Mantell possesses that style, and only lately, in his great impersonation of Shakespeare's *King John*, he exemplified it by such acting as the types of "intensity," "reserved force," and "repression" could never approach,—the production failing to win popular support only because the same excellence was wanting in his associates, who, indeed, provided a spectacle of general incompetence, painful to behold and melancholy to remember. Otis Skinner, in tragedy, has preserved, and, if he pleased, could illustrate, the tradition of it. John Mason, Frank Worthing, N. C. Goodwin, John E. Kellerd, Tyrone Power, Sidney Herbert, John Gilmour, Wilfred Clarke, John Drew, Russ Whytal, and George Arliss, in comedy, have shown the dominant influence of it upon their minds and methods, and have clearly, though variously, demonstrated their capability to use it or to acquire it. When, for example, was a more exquisite embodiment seen, during the present period,—more refined in spirit, more profound in feeling, more delicate yet keenly forcible in expression,—than Mr. Whytal's personation of *Judge Prentice*, in one of the most modern of plays, Augustus Thomas's superb play of "The Witching Hour"? The acceptance accorded to William Faversham's presentment of *King Herod*, even though only a hint of the old tragic fashion appeared in it, signifies the trend of the public mind toward substantial themes and artistic endeavor. Miss Viola Allen, in point of authority, purity of style, and facility and finish of execution, is an actress whose presence would have graced Burton's or Wallack's stage, in the best period of those remarkable institutions,—and, perhaps, that was a period as golden as any in our theatrical history. Miss Blanche Bates has shown the power, the fire, the impetuosity, and the charm that veterans still remember in Charlotte Crampton, Mrs. Bowers,

FOREWORD

Jean Davenport, and Matilda Heron. Miss Julia Marlowe can make actual, and has often done so, the most delicate ideal of romantic womanhood. It is good to believe, and there is comfort in knowing that we *can* believe, that the spirit of romance has not been altogether blighted, notwithstanding the sordid

CLARA MORRIS
IN
"THE SPHINX"

efforts of tradesmen to turn the Theatre into a shop, and notwithstanding the injudicious, not to say pernicious, tattle of the press, making common and prosy the whole mechanism of the stage, and dissipating that glamour of poetic mystery which ought always to be left undisturbed around the actor's profession.

Actors are more numerous in the present period, in America, than ever before in the history of our stage, and, as a class, they possess much and diversified talent. The scope and efficacy of their ministration, however, are restricted by reason of their general subservience to an unsympathetic, inauspicious control. Their affairs, which ought to be exclusively in their own hands, are, to a great extent, in the hands of "middlemen"; persons who contribute nothing, do nothing, and are nothing; persons who, as remarked by Richard Mansfield, sit in arm-chairs, smoke cigars, and grow fat by "booking dates." Expeditious methods of "doing business" are pleasing to consider and are highly commendable, but they are not unusual, certainly they are not startling, and it has not yet been ascertained that expert book-keeping, private wires and convenient "'phones" involve either natural fitness or acquired qualification to direct intellectual forces of vital import to the public welfare. In fact, it has been surmised that theatrical management would be the better for less tape and more talent. Indications, indeed, are not lacking, that this undesirable state of theatrical affairs is becoming appreciated as disastrous to the Theatre, and that actors are beginning to understand that they,— and not the middlemen,—are the producers; that the charm of the stage resides in their faculties, that the value of the Theatre is commensurate only with their attractive ability, and that the profits which accrue from dramatic representation belong to them, and not to janitors and ticket-sellers. Here and there already an actor is visible who insists on managing his own business. Too often, though, the practice still prevails of running with the stream, and many an actor is satisfied,—if he can obtain a good salary,— to abdicate his individuality, to take orders from a blustering, insolent huckster, to play one part for a whole season, or for many successive seasons, and to cast to the winds all care about the improvement of his faculties, the advancement of his profession, or the fulfilment of his duty to the public as an intellectual man exercising an intellectual art. Indeed the obnoxious phrase "art for art's sake" frequently falls with a sneer from lips to which such idle, paltry words should always be strange. Nobody wants "art for art's sake." Art is wanted for the actor's sake, and still more for the sake of his audience,—for if art, whether dramatic or other, does not help mankind, it is worse than useless. Nobody, meanwhile, objects to the honest, legitimate quest of substantial, practical profit. "The laborer is worthy of his hire." The actor should be paid for his acting, and he should be well paid. No worker better deserves his reward than the worker whose toil is directed toward improving the mind, refining the manners, elevating the

FOREWORD

spirit, and thus augmenting the happiness of mankind. This view of the subject impresses tradesmen, the "keepers of theatrical shops," as "visionary," "impractical," "theoretical," "behind the times"; but this is the view that the dramatic profession ought to take of itself; this is the only view that will justify the claim made for it to honor and support; and this is the view that, eventually, it will take of itself, to the expulsion of many money-changers from the temple, and to the correction of many abuses which the Theatre and the Public have too long endured. How well it is entitled to take, and to insist upon, this view of itself, a thoughtful inspection of the lives, the talents, and the achievements of the men and women who have been, and who are, devoted to its service, will make manifest to every thoughtful reader. Intellect, character, ambition, toil, endurance, beauty, manifold accomplishments—those are the lilies and roses in the garland of dramatic biography here woven, which also lacks not the modest violet of humble service and the lowly myrtle of duty well done.

MADAME MODJESKA
AS
LADY MACBETH

MARY ANDERSON
AS
THE COUNTESS

Mr JOHN DREW

JOHN DREW'S career divides itself conveniently into two periods: the first of seventeen years, under the management of Augustin Daly for the greater part of the time, sharing leading honors in that inimitable Daly Theatre quartette—Ada Rehan, Mrs. Gilbert, James Lewis, and himself, —and the second period of the past seventeen years since 1892 as a star under the management of Charles Frohman.

He was born in Philadelphia, in November, 1853. His father, John Drew, was a celebrated comedian and actor of Irish characters, and his mother was one of the famous artists of her period. He went on the stage at twenty and played his first parts at the Arch Street Theatre, Philadelphia, while it was under the management of his mother. It was there that Augustin Daly saw him and engaged him for his New York company.

Mr. Drew made his first appearance in New York at Daly's Fifth Avenue Theatre, February 17, 1875, as Bob Ruggles in "The Big Bonanza." Under this management he played over seventy parts, several of them acted in support of Edwin Booth, Fanny Davenport and Frederick Warde, to whom Mr. Daly loaned his services.

"JACK STRAW"

When the present Daly's Theatre was opened in 1880 Mr. Drew became leading man there and appeared at the head of the company on its visits to London and Paris.

Under Mr. Frohman's management he has on an average appeared in one new play a year since his début as a star at Palmer's Theatre, October 3, 1892, as Paul Blondet in "The Masked Ball," with Maude Adams as his leading woman. The characters and plays in the order of their production have been Frederick Ossia in "The Butterflies," Lord Clivebrook in "The Bauble Shop," John Annesley in "That Imprudent Young Couple," Christopher Colt, Jr., in "Christopher, Jr.," Mr. Kilroy in "The Squire of Dames," Sir Jasper Thorndyke in "Rosemary," Comte de Condale in "A Marriage of Convenience," Dick Rudyard in "One Summer's Day," Sir Christopher Dering in "The Liars," Mr. Parbury in "The Tyranny of Tears," "Richard Carvel," Christopher Bingham in "The Second in Command," Lord Lumley in "The Mummy and the Humming Bird," "Captain Dieppe," "The Duke of Killicrankie," James DeLancey in "DeLancey," Hilary Jesson in "His House in Order," Gerald Eversleigh in "My Wife," "Jack Straw," and George Bullin in "Inconstant George."

"RICHARD CARVEL"

"INCONSTANT GEORGE"

CHRISTOPHER BINGHAM

CHARLES SURFACE

Mr JOHN DREW

Miss Ethel Barrymore

ANGELA MUIR IN "A COUNTRY MOUSE"

"COUSIN KATE"

MADAME TRENTONI IN "CAPTAIN JINKS"

IN adopting the stage Ethel Barrymore must have felt the call of the blood. Her father was Maurice Barrymore, actor and dramatist. Her mother was Georgiana Drew-Barrymore, daughter of the celebrated Mrs. John Drew. Her two uncles, John and Sidney Drew; her cousin, Louise Drew; and her two brothers, Lionel and John Barrymore, are all on the stage to-day. Miss Barrymore was born in Philadelphia in 1878. She made her début under Charles Frohman's direction at the Empire Theatre, in the autumn of 1894, and she has been under his management continually since except during a year spent in England in Sir Henry Irving's company.

Her first rôle was Kate Fennell in "The Bauble Shop" in her Uncle John Drew's support. With him she next played Katherine in "That Imprudent Young Couple," Zoë in "The Squire of Dames," and Priscilla in "Rosemary." Her English debut was made in support of William Gillette as Miss Kittridge in "Secret Service," May 15, 1897, at the Adelphi Theatre, London. At the termination of that play's run she joined Sir Henry Irving on tour and on his return to London, on New Year's Day, 1898, she created Euphrosine in "Peter the Great" at the Lyceum. At the close of that season she returned home and Mr. Frohman cast her in "Catherine" in support of Annie Russell and as Stella de Grex in "His Excellency the Governor" before giving her a stellar position.

Her first character as a star was Madame Trentoni, the American prima donna returning to her native shores, in Clyde Fitch's comedy of the early 70's, "Captain Jinks of the Horse Marines," acted first at the Garrick Theatre, New York, on February 4, 1901, and the breadth and depth of her later creations has not obscured the memory of this altogether charming performance. Her season's routine has since been devoted to light comedies nearly always of English origin or English life. The list includes her admirably conceived boy in "Carrots"; the name part in "Sunday"; "Cousin Kate"; Angela Muir in "A Country Mouse"; Gwendolyn Cobb in "The Painful Predicament of Sherlock Holmes"; Nora in a few performances of "A Doll's House" at the Lyceum Theatre, New York; Mrs. Grey in Barrie's "Alice-Sit-By-the-Fire," which moved an unprofessional critic to remark that he preferred her performance to the play, "not that I like Barrie less but Ethel Barrymore"; Mrs. Jones in "The Silver Box" at the Empire for a few nights in the spring of 1907; and the leading rôles in "Her Sister," "Miss Civilization," and Maugham's "Lady Frederick." A second English experiment was made in the spring of 1904, when she played the title-rôle in Hubert Henry Davies's "Cynthia," at Wyndham's Theatre. She was admired, but the performances were not many. Miss Barrymore's latest rôle is in Sir Arthur Wing Pinero's "Mid-Channel." Early in 1909 she became the wife of Russell G. Colt.

Miss ETHEL BARRYMORE

Copyright 1902 by Burr McIntosh

Mr. E. H. SOTHERN

"DON QUIXOTE"

HEINRICH IN "THE SUNKEN BELL" FRANÇOIS VILLON IN "IF I WERE KING" BENEDICK

"LORD DUNDREARY"

"HAMLET"

E. H. SOTHERN is the son of E. A. "Dundreary" Sothern, and was born December 6, 1859, in New Orleans. He was taken to England when five years old, and received his schooling in Dunchurch, Warwickshire, and in London. It was designed that he should become a painter. But he had other ideas, and he has pursued them with an energy, ambition, and zeal that has resulted in raising him to a high place among contemporary actors. His dramatic career readily divides itself into the period of early struggle, the years at the old Lyceum in Fourth Avenue, and his independent efforts in the realm of tragic and poetic drama.

To the first period belongs his first appearance on the stage as the Cabman, with his father, in "Brother Sam" at the Park Theatre, New York City; brief experiences at the Boston Museum, in John McCullough's Company, two years of miscellaneous service in minor parts in London productions, parts in the American tours of "Called Back," "Lost," "Three Wives to One Husband," "The Fatal Letter," and as leading man with Helen Barry, Estelle Clayton and Helen Dauvray.

He went to the Lyceum as leading man in 1885 and left in 1898, during which time he advanced himself to the rank of a star. At the Lyceum he acted in "One of Our Girls," "A Scrap of Paper," "Met by Chance," "Masks and Faces," "Walda Lamar," "The Love Chase," "The Highest Bidder," in which he made his stellar début; "The Great Pink Pearl," "Editha's Burglar," "Lord Chumley," "The Maister of Woodbarrow," "The Dancing Girl," "Lettarblair," "The Disreputable Mr. Reagan," "Sheridan," "The Victoria Cross," "A Way to Win a Woman," "The Prisoner of Zenda," "An Enemy to the King," "'Change Alley," "The Lady of Lyons," "The Adventure of Lady Ursula," "A Colonial Girl," and "An Unwarranted Intrusion."

Subsequently he played D'Artagnan, "The Song of the Sword," Heinrich in "The Sunken Bell," and "Drifted Apart." At the Garden Theatre, September 17, 1900, he acted Hamlet for the first time, and this performance marked the change in his efforts toward a higher plane. He followed it with impersonations of Richard Lovelace, François Villon, King Robert of Sicily, and Markheim. Charles Frohman brought Mr. Sothern and Miss Julia Marlowe together in 1904 for a joint starring tour, and during their intermittent association since they have acted in "Romeo and Juliet," "Much Ado About Nothing," "Hamlet," "The Taming of the Shrew," "The Merchant of Venice," "Twelfth Night," "Jeanne d'Arc,""The Sunken Bell," and "John the Baptist." Mr. Sothern starred alone for two seasons, during 1907 and 1908, playing in Laurence Irving's "The Fool Hath Said," an uncommonly delightful revival of his father's rôle in "Lord Dundreary," and the best composed performance of his career as Don Quixote in Paul Kester's dramatization of Cervantes's masterpiece. In the performance of "Antony and Cleopatra," with which The New Theatre was dedicated, Mr. Sothern acted Antony. He has written much verse and four plays: "I Love, Thou Lovest, He Loves," "The Luncheon at Nick's," "Never Trouble Trouble Till Trouble Troubles You," and "The Light That Lies in Woman's Eyes."

Mr. E. H. SOTHERN

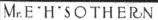

MISS MABEL TALIAFERRO

LOVEY MARY
IN
"MRS. WIGGS OF THE CABBAGE PATCH"

DOLLY
IN
"YOU NEVER CAN TELL"

MABEL TALIAFERRO is a remarkable young artist from whatever point one views her career. She has been playing conspicuous and in many cases leading parts in plays since she was two and a half years of age and enjoys the distinction of being the youngest star in America. She might retire now and her career of activity and accomplishment would be notable for one twice her years. To all her characters she has brought girlish charm, rare poetic sense, a frail, delicate beauty and a genuine aptitude for the stage.

Miss Taliaferro was born in New York City, May 21, 1887, and began to act Baby Bascome in "Blue Jeans" two and a half years afterwards. At five years she was one of the principals in "Patent Applied For," and before she was seven she acted in the companies of Andrew Mack and Chauncey Olcott. The part that brought attention to her as more than a mere precocious child actress was her exquisite Esther in "Children of the Ghetto" in 1889. This rôle took her abroad, where she created the adorable Fairie Child in Yates' "The Land of Heart's Desire," which she played under the author's direction before the leading literary organizations of Ireland.

Her performances have been so genuine and so mature in their art that it is some time since Miss Taliaferro has been thought of as a child actress, yet she created Lovey Mary in "Mrs. Wiggs of the Cabbage Patch" before she was sixteen. Then followed Dolly Clandon in "You Never Can Tell," her long tour as Nance Olden in "In the Bishop's Carriage," a trip to Australia in support of William Collier, and, on her return, her fine performance of Pippa in Browning's "Pippa Passes" at the Majestic Theatre.

Stellar honors came to her in 1907 when she created the title rôle in "Polly of the Circus," which she followed in 1909 with Madelaine in Booth Tarkington and Harry L. Wilson's "Springtime." She is studying Parthenia in "Ingomar" and "King Rene's Daughter" for her repertoire, which is perhaps indicative of the direction and scope which she wishes to give to her career.

NANCE OLDEN
IN
"IN THE BISHOP'S CARRIAGE"

MADELAINE
IN
"SPRINGTIME"

MISS MABEL TALIAFERRO

"POLLY OF THE CIRCUS"

Mr. KYRLE BELLEW

IN "THE THIEF"

ROMEO

ANTONY

"RAFFLES"

IN "A GENTLEMAN OF FRANCE"

HAROLD KYRLE BELLEW has had quite the most nomadic and varied career of any of our leading actors. He was born at Prescot, Lancashire. England, March 28, 1857. His father was a clergyman and public reader. He first entered the English merchant marine, but soon went to Australia, where he was a lecturer, a gold digger, a writer, and finally an actor. His first part was Eglinton in "Turn Him Out," and he made his début at Solferino, in Australia, in 1874.

The next year he returned to England and acted there continuously in the principal theatres and companies, including Irving's, for ten years. He came to America in 1882, but returned without playing. It was three years later that he made his American début, playing Hubert in "In His Power" at Wallack's. He remained two seasons and returned to England in 1888 and formed a partnership with Cora Urquhart Potter. They were joint stars almost uninterruptedly for ten years. Together they played in America, Australia, India, and nearly every city in the world where there were audiences who understood English. During this time Mr. Bellew made thirty productions and acted one of the principal rôles in each. His notable performances were Romeo, Orlando, Lucien in "Françillon," Marat in "Charlotte Corday," and Leander in his own version of "Hero and Leander."

After appearing in London as Cosmo in "The Jest," as Olivier in "Robespierre" with Irving and Terry, and as Rafael in "The Ghetto," Mr. Bellew abandoned the stage temporarily in 1899 and returned to Australia and accumulated a considerable fortune in gold-mining. He revisited America in 1901 and has since been applauded as one of the really gifted artists of the stage, giving superior interpretations of every type of character in poetic and realistic drama.

Since his return to the stage his characters have been Gaston de Marsac in "A Gentleman of France"; Romeo, Chevalier de Vaudray, and Young Marlow in "all-star" revivals of "Romeo and Juliet," "The Two Orphans," and "She Stoops to Conquer"; "Raffles"; Jacques Bernez in "The Sacrament of Judas"; Brigadier Gerard in Conan Doyle's play of that name; Richard Voysin in "The Thief"; and Edward Thursfield in "The Builder of Bridges."

Mr KYRLE BELLEW

MISS ADELINE GENÉE

A T a time when it was supposed that the line of great ballet dancers was broken there suddenly appeared on the New York stage a young Dane, Adeline Genée "of the twinkling feet," who has proved herself a veritable artist and a sister of Taglioni, Ellsler, and Grisi. Her effort has not been to give new form and meaning to the dance, as have several contemporaries, so much as to demonstrate the beauty and charm of traditional forms when given their perfect expression.

Miss Genée was born in Aartrus, Ytland, Denmark. She was taught to dance by her aunt, Mlle. Zimmerman, herself a dancer, and her uncle, Alexander Genée, who was the original producer of Delibes' "Copelia." She began to prepare for her career when five years of age and made her début when in her seventeenth year at the principal theatre of Copenhagen. Engagements at the Berlin Grand Opera and in Munich followed, and in 1897 she reached the Empire Music Hall, London. She was a success, then a vogue and developed into an institution. For ten years she danced on no other stage, except during the run of "The Little Michus" at Daly's, where special dances were interpolated for her. She has appeared "by command" before numerous royalties in London and in Copenhagen.

In 1907, she came to America and made her début at the New York Theatre in a musical comedy, "The Soul Kiss," written especially to introduce her dances, and was proclaimed "a Tetrazzini of the toes." In the fall of 1909 she presented new dances in "The Silver Star," and in addition she has in this production, for the first time in her life, a speaking part.

NED TRENT IN "THE CALL OF THE NORTH"

"STRONGHEART"

Mr. ROBERT EDESON

DUKE OF HERMANOS IN "THE NOBLE SPANIARD"

DUNCAN IRVING IN "CLASSMATES"

ROBERT EDESON went on the stage as the result of a wager. He was not, however, an entire stranger to the theatre by any means, for his father, George R. Edeson, was a well-known comedian and stage manager, and his first money was earned as an assistant in the box office of Colonel Sinn's Park Theatre in Brooklyn. While he was there, Cora Tanner was to produce "Fascination" at the Park Theatre, but one of her company, cast to play a minor part, became ill and young Edeson volunteered to act the part. Colonel Sinn offered to bet him one hundred dollars he could not. But he did, and he was paid this sum for his début. This happened in 1887, when he was nineteen years old.

Thereafter he played many parts under many managers, sometimes in New York City, sometimes on tour, but always conscientiously and with a nice adaptability to direct, manly characters, and from year to year his popularity advanced steadily. From "Fascination" he went into a minor company which Augustin Daly was sending on tour in "A Night Off," and thence for a year into "A Dark Secret." After a variety of other engagements, which gave him little besides experience, he became a member of Charles Hoyt's Madison Square Theatre Company, and played with them in "That Cowboy," "The Charms of Music," "A Modest Model," and "A Mere Pretense."

It was only a step up street from the Madison Square Theatre to the Empire, but it was a stride ahead for young Edeson when he began to play juveniles in Charles Frohman's Stock Company in December, 1894. For three years he had conspicuous parts in all the new plays, and when Maude Adams made her début as a star, he became her leading man and played the name part in Barrie's "The Little Minister." He was now coming in to a position in the theatre, and during the few years following he created the parts of Captain Carew in Marshall's "His Excellency the Governor" at the Lyceum Theatre; David Brandon in Zangwill's "Children of the Ghetto" at the Herald Square, and shortly afterwards in the same play at the Adelphi Theatre, London; leading parts in "The Greatest Thing in the World," and "The Moment of Death" at Wallack's; and Edward Warden in the first performance of Clyde Fitch's "The Climbers" at the Bijou Theatre, December 17, 1900.

The next time he was seen in a new part was as a star at the Savoy Theatre in March, 1902, in Richard Harding Davis's "Soldiers of Fortune." Since then, his new plays have been "The Rector's Garden," "Ranson's Folly," "Strongheart," "The Sinner," "Classmates," "The Call of the North," "The Noble Spaniard," "The Outpost" in one act, and "A Man's A Man."

Miss BILLIE BURKE

THE trail of Billie Burke's career requires quite a geographical sprint. She was born in Washington, D. C., in 1886; received her education in France; toured through Austria, Russia, Germany and France when in her mid-teens; then raised herself to a high place among London musical comediennes, and returned home to become almost immediately popular as a star in every city she has visited.

Miss Burke was christened Ethel, but she wished to perpetuate the name of her father, an actor affectionately known as Billie Burke, and so for professional purposes she took the tripping alliterative trade-mark. Her prominence is not entirely the accident which some people may imagine it to be. It is contributed to, of course, by her youth and beauty, but it is grounded in a zealous ambition and hard study.

She was taken to England when twelve years old to improve her voice and crossed to France to add languages to her accomplishments. Her beginnings before the European public were made as a singer of light popular songs. London first saw her at the Pavilion, after which she was obscured in provincial pantomime at Glasgow and Sheffield. Returning to the British metropolis she was engaged by George Edwardes for his light musical productions, and she soon rose to a leading position through the series which included "The School Girl," "The Duchess of Dantzic," "The Blue Moon," the Coliseum revue of 1906, and "The Belle of Mayfair."

Her success in this branch of her profession only stimulated her to honors in another, so she sought an engagement in straight comedy, and in the spring of 1906 she appeared as leading woman for Charles Hawtrey in "Mr. George" at the Vaudeville Theatre. It was her succeeding success as Stella in "Mrs. Ponderbury's Past" at the same theatre that induced Charles Frohman to bring her to America as John Drew's leading woman, in "My Wife" at the Empire. In 1908 she became a star in "Love Watches," giving a bewitching performance as Jacqueline. She followed this in the name part in W. Somerset Maugham's "Mrs. Dot." Behind the springtime of Billie Burke's laughing eyes there is a secret; it is the intense inevitable regret of the pretty comedienne that she is not playing tragedy.

TRIXIE IN "MY WIFE"

Miss BILLIE BURKE

JAQUELINE IN "LOVE WATCHES"

JAQUELINE IN "LOVE WATCHES"

IN
"A VIRGINIA COURTSHIP"

FALSTAFF

LORD HARDCASTLE
IN "SHE STOOPS TO CONQUER"

Mr WILLIAM H CRANE

WILLIAM H. CRANE'S audiences have always known him as an old man, but his friends think of him only as young. His very first part on the stage, acted in Mrs. Holman's company at Utica, N. Y., July 13, 1863, was that of an old notary in "The Daughter of the Regiment," although at the time he was only eighteen years of age. His gallery has disclosed the amiable, the shrewd, the gullible, the gay, but seldom the wicked type of middle-aged or old man. The public are so accustomed to like Mr. Crane's characters that not long ago when he acted an unsympathetic French plutocrat in "Business is Business," an uncommonly fine performance did not elicit entire forgiveness for the imposition his public felt had been put upon them by being robbed of their laugh.

In Mrs. Holman's little company Crane sang, acted and danced, but he soon graduated to a fixed line as a low comedian in support of Alice Oates. One of the celebrated parts that attaches to his earlier years is Le Blanc, of which he was the original in "Evangeline." He appeared in several musical companies, but finally created the part of Col. M. T. Elevator, in a comedy called "Our Boarding House," produced at the Park Theatre, New York, in January, 1877. He met Stuart Robson in this company, and the sequel is significant in the annals of American comedy.

Robson and Crane two years later formed a partnership to act in American comedies and for ten years their productions were the vogue. Among the comedies in which they played together were "The Comedy of Errors," in which they acted the two Dromios, "Our Bachelors," "Flats and Sharps," "Twelfth Night," "The Cherubs," and the unforgettable "The Henrietta," in which Crane played Nicholas Vanalstyne and Robson was Bertie the Lamb.

Crane headed his own company in January, 1890, when he made his hit as Senator Hannibal Rivers in "The Senator." His succeeding comedies have been "On Probation," "For Money," "The American Minister," "Brother John," "The Merry Wives of Windsor," in which he acted Falstaff, "The Pacific Mail," "His Wife's Father," "The Governor of Kentucky," "The Fool of Fortune," "A Virginia Courtship," "His Last Appearance," "His Honor the Mayor," "Worth a Million," "The Head of the Family," "Peter Stuyvesant," "A Rich Man's Son," "David Harum," "The Spenders," "Business is Business," "The American Lord," "The Price of Money," and "Father and the Boys." Mr. Crane has also acted Sir Anthony Absolute and Old Hardcastle in all-star revivals of "The Rivals" and "She Stoops to Conquer."

SIR ANTHONY ABSOLUTE
IN
"THE RIVALS"

IN
"FATHER AND THE BOYS"

"DAVID HARUM"

Mr WILLIAM H CRANE

ISADORE LECHAT
IN
"BUSINESS IS BUSINESS"

IN
"THE SENATOR"

"DAVID HARUM"

MISS "FRITZI" SCHEFF

"THE PRIMA DONNA"

THERE are instances of actresses who have abandoned tragedy for comedy, romance for realism, singing for acting, comic opera for grand opera, but Fritzi Scheff furnishes probably the first example of a grand opera artiste who has stepped successfully from the classic plane of Mozart and Wagner to the popular plane of Herbert and Suppé. After establishing herself in Europe as a light soprano of uncommon temperament, she came to the Metropolitan Opera House, and from that celebrated stage passed gracefully into a position in the front rank of American comic opera prima donnas.

Fritzi Scheff is the daughter of Dr. Jager and Hortense Scheff. She was born in the year 1879 in Vienna, where her father was a physician and her mother was a prima donna at the Imperial Opera House. As late as 1906 Mme. Scheff-Jager was singing in grand opera in Frankfort. Miss Scheff made her musical studies in Dresden and Frankfort. She made her début in the latter place in 1897, singing Juliet in Gounod's "Romeo and Juliet." Among the rôles which she added to her repertoire during these two years were the prima donna parts in Gounod's "Faust," "Cavalleria Rusticana," "La Bohème," and "Mignon." Maurice Grau, the director of the Metropolitan Opera House, heard her sing in Munich in 1900 and engaged her for his company. She found herself at once in the most distinguished assembly of artists that this great stage has ever known. Others in the company while she sang there were Eames, Sembrich, Melba, Nordica, Calvé, Jean and Édouard de Reszke, Caruso, Lassalle, and Plançon. Yet she maintained herself in a popular, if not a preeminent, position, and was much applauded by the public for her cleverness and vivacity. During three years at the Metropolitan she sang in "Fidelio," "Lohengrin," "The Flying Dutchman," "Die Walküre," Musetta in "La Bohème," Zerlina in "Don Giovanni," Cherubino in "The Marriage of Figaro," Papagena in "The Magic Flute," Nedda in "Pagliacci," and Asa in "Manru."

Her début in comic opera, which she at once sang in English, was made in Washington, November 9, 1903, in Victor Herbert's "Babette." She has since sung in "The Two Roses," which was a musical version of "She Stoops to Conquer"; "Fatinitza," "Giroflé-Girofla," "Boccaccio," "M'lle Modiste," and "The Prima Donna."

"M'LLE MODISTE"

IN "THE TWO ROSES"

Miss FRITZI SCHEFF

SYDNEY CARTON IN "THE ONLY WAY"

"D'ARCY OF THE GUARDS"

MR. HENRY MILLER

EPHEN GHENT IN "THE GREAT DIVIDE"

THOSE close to Henry Miller know that, much as the public is indebted to him for the pleasure his own fine characterizations have given them, they are, in recent years, since he has been active as the director of his own stage, under quite as much obligation for his influence on the interpretation and realization of the characters and ensemble about him. There are some who contend that Mr. Miller is the greatest living stage manager. He has done much to support this contention, for not only has his judgment searched out new plays with values along unconventional lines, but his gifts are pronounced for creating atmosphere and reality, less with scenery, lights and furniture than with the revelation of the psychology of the drama and the actor. Correct environment subordinated to the full revelation of the characters in the drama is the artistic keynote of his productions.

Mr. Miller is only an American by adoption. He was born in England and went to school in Canada. His early years in the theatre, which he entered for a career first when a lad of eighteen, were spent under the influence of C. W. Couldock and Dion Boucicault, to whom he renders appreciative homage. His first part was the bleeding sergeant in "Macbeth" at the Grand Opera House, Toronto, early in 1878. Before the end of the season he had worked his way into leading parts.

A varied, valuable experience followed during the next fifteen years. He played leading parts with Helena Modjeska, Adelaide Neilson, Marie Wainwright and the Lyceum Stock Company, and was the original or first American embodiment of Howard in "Young Mrs. Winthrop," Robert Gray in "The Wife," Clement Hale in "Sweet Lavender," Mark Field in "Honor Bright," Colonel Kerchival West in "Shenandoah," Alfred Hastings in "All the Comforts of Home," Carroll Cotton Vanderstyle in "The Merchant," the Earl of Leicester in "Amy Robsart," "Frederic Lemaitre" in Clyde Fitch's one-act play of that name, and Dick Wellington in "His Wedding Day."

Mr. Miller's first permanent association was as leading man at the Empire Theatre, which he entered in 1893, and the importance and expertness of his performances there make it seem as if he had remained longer than three years. At the Empire he played Mr. Owen in "Liberty Hall," Paul Kirkland in "The Younger Son," Ted Morris in "The Councillor's Wife," Mr. Brabazon in "Sowing the Wind," James Ffolliott in "Gudgeons," David Remon in "The Masqueraders," Harold Wynn in "John-a-Dreams," John Worthing in "The Importance of Being Earnest," Michael Faversham in "Michael and His Lost Angel," Stephen d'Acosta in "A Woman's Reason" and Rudolph in "Bohemia."

He began to star in 1897 and his direction has given significance and force to every element of the productions in which he has appeared. Among the important plays he has presented are "Heartsease," "The Master," "The Only Way," "D'Arcy of the Guards," "The Taming of Helen," "Joseph Entangled," "Grierson's Way," "Young Fernald," "The Great Divide" and "The Faith Healer." During four summers he directed and acted with Margaret Anglin in notable revivals in San Francisco, and he placed her before the American public as a star in "Zira" and "The Great Divide." Mr. Miller has produced many plays in which he did not act, among which are "Brown of Harvard," Percy Mackaye's "Mater," Robert Browning's "Pippa Passes," Robert Davis's "The Family" and C. R. Kennedy's "The Servant in the House." In the summer of 1909 he acted in London with distinguished success.

MR. HENRY MILLER

"THE LADY OF LYONS"

Miss MARY MANNERING

"BARBARA FRIETCHIE"

WHILE in England in 1896, searching for a leading lady to supplant Georgia Cayvan in the affections of the old Lyceum's clientele, Daniel Frohman heard of a beautiful young girl named Florence Friend playing on tour in "The Late Mr. Costello." He found her at the Grand, Islington, and after viewing one performance he engaged her to come to America. From the time she stepped on the steamer and the home country disappeared below the horizon the career of Florence Friend was closed. She became Mary Mannering and America knows her by no other name.

Miss Mannering studied for the stage under Herman Vezin. Her first engagement was with Kyrle Bellew and Mrs. Potter while they were on tour in England, and she made her début as Zela in Mr. Bellew's "Hero and Leander" at Manchester, May 9, 1892, when she was fifteen years old, and she acted in London soon after under the same auspices. For four years she divided her activities between metropolis and provinces, rising finally to leading parts before she left England.

Her début at the Lyceum was made as Leonie in "The Courtship of Leonie," November 20, 1896, and during the remaining years that the Lyceum stood she maintained her position there at the head of the company in the productions of "The Late Mr. Costello," "The First Gentleman of Europe," "The Mayflower," "The Princess and the Butterfly," "The Tree of Knowledge," "Trelawney of the Wells," "Americans at Home" and "John Ingerfield." Thence she went to Daly's Theatre in the spring of 1900, when that house was under Daniel Frohman's management, and acted in "The Ambassador" and "The Interrupted Honeymoon."

Miss Mannering began to star in the autumn of that year. Her first play was the dramatization of Paul Leicester Ford's story of Colonial days, "Janice Meredith," and her popularity was at once widespread. Since then she has appeared in "White Roses," as Pauline in "The Lady of Lyons," as Geraldine in Clyde Fitch's "The Stubbornness of Geraldine," as Harriet Baird in "Harriet's Honeymoon," in "Nancy Stair," as Lady Alithea Frobisher in "The Walls of Jericho," as Beatrice in "The House of Silence," as Betsy in "Glorious Betsy," in "The Struggle," "A House of Cards," "Step by Step," "The Truants," "The Independent Miss Gower," and "Kiddie," subsequently renamed "A Man's World."

Miss MARY MANNERING

JANICE MEREDITH IN "NANCY STAIR"

MISS MARIE DORO

LIKE a number of other popular young actresses, some of them stars as she is, Marie Doro had her stage beginnings in the chorus of musical comedy. She reached the distinction of a character all her own while playing in a musical comedy company in San Francisco in 1903. She went to New York the same year and appeared as Rosalba Peppercorn in "The Billionaire," in support of the late Jerome Sykes, and as Nancy Lowly in "The Girl from Kay's."

Charles Frohman saw possibilities of higher things from her, and has directed her movements since. She made her first appearance in drama as Lady Millicent in Barrie's "Little Mary" at the Empire, January 4, 1904. When Mrs. Gilbert made her début as a star in her eighty-second year, Miss Doro played Dora in Fitch's "Granny," and in January, 1905, she created the title rôle in "Friquet" at the Savoy. That play was not a success, and she went to London in William Collier's company to play Lucy Sheridan in "The Dictator," and she remained to create the title rôle in Gillette's "Clarice" and to act Alice Faulkner with the actor-dramatist when he presented "Sherlock Holmes" in the British capital. That year of 1905 was a busy one for Miss Doro, for at the close of Mr. Gillette's brief London season, they hurried home and played "Clarice" together on tour during 1906 and 1907. Her next appearance was as Carlotta, the little semi-English Syrian girl, in W. J. Locke's comedy, "The Morals of Marcus," at the Criterion Theatre, November 18, 1907. After a long starring tour in this play, she returned to the same theatre in March, 1909, and appeared as Benjamine Monnier in "The Richest Girl," but soon resumed her tour in Locke's comedy.

Miss Doro is a young actress of piquant beauty, marked personality and rare expressiveness of countenance. She has been conspicuous on the stage only a short time, but she has steadily increased the number of her admirers.

MISS MARIE DORO

IN "CLARICE"

CARLOTTA
IN
"THE MORALS OF MARCUS"

IN "A ROMANCE OF ATHLONE"
Copyright 1904 by Sarony

EDMUND BURKE

MR. CHAUNCEY OLCOTT

IN "RAGGED ROBIN"

THERE is probably not in America another actor who has so faithful an individual following as Chauncey Olcott. It used to be said that Sol Smith Russell drew people to the theatre who would go to see no one else. "Ben-Hur" has been made one of the most largely attended plays of the past ten years by others than regular theatre-goers.

Mr. Olcott, likewise, has his own clientele, augmented to be sure by a large section of the regular patrons of the theatre. Rarely does he appear that the theatre is not filled in every part. He has made a specialty of romantic and sentimental Irish comedy and in the course of each play he sings several songs of his own composition.

The name under which he is so widely known was adopted by him for professional purposes. His own name is Chancellor John Olcott. He was born in Buffalo in 1860 and attended the public schools there. His first dozen years on the stage were not at all prophetic of his later career. He began his life in the theatre in 1880 as a ballad singer with Emerson and Hooley's Minstrels and sang afterwards with Haverly's and Carncross' Minstrels.

It was but a step into light opera and in 1886 he sang Pablo in "Pepita" at the Union Square Theatre. Lillian Russell sang the title rôle. He was with Denman Thompson in "The Old Homestead" from 1888 to 1890, when he became leading tenor with the Duff Opera Company, and sang Nanki-Poo in "The Mikado" and Ralph Rackstraw in "H. M. S. Pinafore." The next season he appeared in London at the Criterion Theatre in "Miss Decima" and "Blue-Eyed Susan."

Up to that time W. J. Scanlon had been the idol of the large section of the public who love sentimental Irish plays with a romantic singing hero. On his death, his manager, Augustus Pitou, engaged Mr. Olcott to star in this type of play and his success was instant and he has maintained it. He has acted in a new piece each season. The well remembered ones are "Mavourneen," "The Irish Artist," "The Minstrel of Clare," "Sweet Inniscarra," "A Romance of Athlone," "Garrett O'Magh," "Old Limerick Town," "Terence," "Edmund Burke," "Eileen Asthore," "O'Neill of Derry," and "Ragged Robin."

MISS BERTHA GALLAND

BERTHA GALLAND is a beautiful young star who rose rapidly to a position of prominence, made herself admired and popular, and awaits the proper vehicle to carry her further along in the career of her ambitions. Her demonstrated gifts are virtually all for romantic comedy. Her first year on the stage was devoted to a starring tour through New England as Juliet and the red-handed Queen of Scotland. This was in 1897. The next year she co-starred with Joseph Haworth and added Ophelia to her provincial repertoire.

It was after these brief experiences that she came to New York and presented herself for metropolitan favor as the Princess Ottalie in "The Pride of Jennico" with James K. Hackett at the Criterion Theatre, March 6, 1900. She received approval in no stinted measure. She remained Mr. Hackett's leading woman for two years. It was but a step to a position at the head of her own company. This was accomplished September 10, 1901, at the old Lyceum Theatre, when she appeared as Iseult in "The Forest Lovers." Her appearances in this play were interrupted the next month, but only temporarily, by her playing of Pansy de Castro in "The Love Match," as she starred as Iseult for a year, following it with Esmeralda in a dramatization of Victor Hugo's "Notre Dame." At the head of a Washington stock company during the summer of 1903 she played Lady Teazle and Juliet.

Miss Galland's charms and gifts were best displayed, however, as capricious Dorothy Vernon in Paul Kester's successful romantic comedy, "Dorothy Vernon of Haddon Hall," which delighted her audiences in all parts of the country during two long seasons. Beginning in the fall of 1905, David Belasco directed her on a tour of the country in "Sweet Kitty Bellairs." Two years of absence from the stage followed, owing to her inability to secure a starring vehicle. Miss Galland reappeared in 1909, acting Eve in "The Return of Eve" in New York and through the country.

IN "THE CASE OF REBELLIOUS SUSAN"

Mr. Herbert Kelcey

IN "THE AMAZONS"

IN "THE HEART OF MARYLAND"

I**N** his self-revelations on the stage, Herbert Kelcey has always been correct. His dress has been correct, though far removed from that of a fop; his deportment has been correct, without a trace of affectation; and his acting has been correct, with a niceness which has commended him as one of the most finished of our actors of modern patrician rôles.

Mr. Kelcey is an Englishman, and he had his early stage experiences in his own country. His debut was made at Brighton in "Flirtation" in 1877. He roughed it in the provincial theatres for three years and then reached the London stage. Two years later he came to America and made his first appearance in New York, at Wallack's Theatre, as Philip Radley in "Taken from Life." His early engagements were all at Wallack's, the Fifth Avenue, and the Madison Square Theatres, which were the fashionable stages of the eighties. During this time he was the original in America of many interesting characters. Among them were Count Orloff in Sardou's "Diplomacy," and the Spider in "The Silver King."

When the Lyceum was the first stock company in America Mr. Kelcey was its leading man. He created the principal rôles at the little house in Fourth Avenue for nine consecutive seasons from 1887 to 1896. Among the plays which he helped to make popular were "The Great Pink Pearl," "The Wife," "Sweet Lavender," "The Charity Ball," "The Idler," "Nerves," "Lady Bountiful," "Squire Kate," "The Gray Mare," "The Guardsman," "The Amazons," "The Case of Rebellious Susan," "An Ideal Husband," "The Home Secretary," and "The Benefit of the Doubt." With Mr. Kelcey in this company were Georgia Cayvan, Effie Shannon, Mrs. Whiffen, Mr. and Mrs. Charles Walcot, Isabel Irving, May Robson, W. J. Le Moyne, Fritz Williams, Nelson Wheatcroft, and many others of subsequent high position.

While at the Lyceum Mr. Kelcey found the continuity of well-dressed, correct-mannered, even-tempered society parts monotonous, and he sought a wider field of expression in 1896. His first part off that stage was Alan Kendrick, in support of Mrs. Carter, in "The Heart of Maryland," and he was next seen in "A Coat of Many Colors." After an absence of only two years from the Lyceum stage he reappeared among his familiar surroundings as a star with Miss Effie Shannon, in Clyde Fitch's "The Moth and the Flame," April 11, 1898. Since that date these two players have headed their own company and have made themselves popular in all parts of the country. They have appeared in these plays: "My Lady Dainty," "My Daughter-in-Law," "Manon Lescaut," "Her Lord and Master," "Sherlock Holmes," "Taps," "The Lightning Conductor," "The Daughters of Men," "The Walls of Jericho," and "The Thief."

MISS ROSE STAHL

PATRICIA O'BRIEN IN "THE CHORUS LADY"

ROSE STAHL is known from one end of the country to the other for her singularly amusing performance of Patricia O'Brien in "The Chorus Lady." Nearly ten years ago James Forbes wrote the one-act sketch of this name, and Miss Stahl used it with immense favor in vaudeville. Though it had not worn out its life in this form, he elaborated the story into a four-act play, using his original material largely in the second act, and Miss Stahl repeated her hit as Patricia in the longer play in 1906, and in this form she has played "The Chorus Lady" ever since.

There seems to be no diminution of her favor, and there would appear to be an indefinite future before a comedy of so much reality and diversion. Phoebe Davies played Anna Moore in "'Way Down East" eleven years. Lewis Morrison played Mephistopheles for twenty years. Charles L. Davis acted "Alvin Joslyn" nearly all of a long life. James O'Neill played "The Count of Monte Cristo" over five thousand times. Kate Claxton equalled this record with "The Two Orphans." Denman Thompson began to act Uncle Joshua Whitcomb in vaudeville in 1875 and he has acted that character every one of the thirty-five years since. It is possible "The Chorus Lady" is in the springtime of its year.

Miss Stahl began her stage career under Charles Frohman's management in small parts on tour. Before she found the delectable Patricia she had an active career in stock and travelling companies. It was a rough-and-ready experience, but manifestly it taught her human nature and a secure technique. She followed this with a longer period in every line of parts in permanent companies in Philadelphia, Columbus, and Rochester. Her next experiments were as a star in "An American Gentleman," "Janice Meredith," and other plays. When she secured Mr. Forbes's little sketch she went into vaudeville and has been prosperous and conspicuous as "The Chorus Lady" ever since in both America and England.

MADAME NAZIMOVA

THE career of Alla Nazimova presents an interesting variation on the story of those artists whom Europe has cast into the melting-pot of the American stage. Tommaso Salvini, Sarah Bernhardt, and Eleanor Duse came in the blazing light of a recognized greatness which this country could not patronize with discovery. None of them remained even to learn English. Bohemia sent Fanny Janauschek in the full flower of her career, though our own tongue was the solvent which assimilated her permanently here. Young Alexander Salvini came in the reflected light of his celebrated father. Even Helena Modjeska had a name to conjure with before she reached these shores.

Nazimova came here in the fall of 1905, as the leading support of a Russian actor, Paul Orleneff, and appeared unheralded and inconspicuously at the Criterion Theatre in a repertoire of unknown plays in her native tongue. The appreciation of the few who saw her at once leaped even these bars. Henry Miller offered to star her if she would learn English, of which she did not then know six words. This was in May, 1906. Six months later she made her début in English at the Princess Theatre, with only an interesting trace of accent, and her performance of Hedda Gabler made a deep impression.

This interesting woman was born on May 22, 1879, in Yalta, Crimea, on the Black Sea. She was taken to Geneva when very young. There, with a Russian's talent for tongues, she soon learned to speak French and German fluently and to play the violin. But, when at twelve years of age she returned home to make her first public appearance as a violinist, she discovered she had forgotten her native language and had to learn to speak Russian all over again. Her musical talents were so promising that she was sent in 1892 to the Conservatory at Odessa to study the violin, but instead she chose the dramatic course, and when she graduated she won the gold medal. Stanisloffsky, a great Russian stage director, was in charge of the Artistic Theatre in Odessa at the time and, while she studied, she appeared as a supernumerary on his stage. The next year she began her professional career as leading woman of a theatre in the city of Kostroma in the North of Russia, and is said to have played as many as two hundred parts in a twelvemonth, the range covering rather more than Polonius's catalogue.

She reached St. Petersburg in 1903 and was seen in the leading rôles in "Zaza," "Trilby," "Camille," "The Second Mrs. Tanqueray," "Hedda Gabler," "Magda," and other plays of this highly seasoned order. With Paul Orleneff she left Russia in 1904 to play the interdicted "The Chosen People," in Berlin and London, and adding other plays to their repertoire she reached New York with the results already recited. Her English repertoire now includes "Hedda Gabler," "A Doll's House," "The Master Builder," Robert Bracco's "Countess Coquette," Owen Johnson's "The Comet," and Brandon Tynan's "The Passion Flower."

MADAME NAZIMOVA

IN "THE MAN FROM HOME"

MR. WILLIAM HODGE

IN "SAG HARBOR"

IN "EIGHTEEN MILES FROM HOME"

WILLIAM HODGE'S performance of Daniel Vorhees Pike in Booth Tarkington and Harry Leon Wilson's play "The Man From Home" has placed this interesting comedian beyond the picket line of musical comedy. His character drawing is broad without being exaggerated, it indicates one who observes and appreciates human nature, and he has disclosed a broad versatility rather than a fixed style. His comedy belongs in plays where the denotement is subtle however rich the fun. Yet, in spite of repeated demonstration, the musical comedy has had him in camp at least half of his dozen years on the stage.

His beginning in the theatre was made in 1898 with the Rogers Brothers in their first starring venture, "A Reign of Error." When James A. Herne was looking about for types for his Long Island play, "Sag Harbor," he one day happened on a tall, lank, sandy-haired young man lounging before his boarding-house on a cross street near Broadway. He fitted exactly Mr. Herne's mental picture of Freeman Whitmarsh, the village man-of-all-work, and introducing himself he was delighted to find the young man was an actor and had some experience. It was this casual discovery of William Hodge that led to the happy hit he made as Whitmarsh.

He created another droll bucolic gem in E. E. Kidder's "Sky Farm," in 1902, as the village rustic dodging the widow. The next season he appeared again in musical comedy. This time it was in George Ade's "Peggy From Paris." This was a brief interlude, however, for he was soon on the crest of a secure success as Mr. Stubbins in Alice Hegan Rice's "Mrs. Wiggs of the Cabbage Patch," by many regarded as the best expression of his skill as a generic comedian. During the two years in which he acted Mr. Stubbins he devoted his leisure to writing a play for himself. He called it "Eighteen Miles From Home," and it was produced at the beginning of the season of 1905.

That season proved the most varied season of his career, for after his trial as actor-dramatist he was soon back in musical comedy again, first in "The White Cat" and later in "The Tourist." Throughout the following season he was a member of Joseph Weber's company in "Dream City." His next appearance was as Pike, the Kokomo man in Italy, in "The Man From Home."

MRS. HOWARD JEFFRIES, SR.
IN "THE THIRD DEGREE"

Miss GRACE FILKINS

MRS. HOWARD JEFFRIES, SR.
IN "THE THIRD DEGREE"

GRACE FILKINS is a name which theatre-goers have come during the past few years to associate with an engaging performance of whatever character she may play. Her recent appearances have not been many, for she is removed from the necessity of acting and appears only when an alluring opportunity invites her. In private life Miss Filkins is the wife of Rear-Admiral Marix of the United States navy.

She was born in Philadelphia and when a girl she became a member of Haverly's Juvenile Pinafore Company and sang and acted the part of Josephine, the Captain's daughter. The grace and charm of this performance commended her to Colonel John A. McCaull, who at the time had the famous McCaull Opera Company, and he engaged her. She made her New York début in his company August 30, 1886, playing at Wallack's Theatre in "Josephine Sold by Her Sisters."

Miss Filkins crossed the street to Daly's the November following and there laid the foundations of a comedy and dramatic career with Ada Rehan, Mrs. Gilbert, John Drew, James Lewis and the other celebrated players under Augustin Daly. Her first appearance was as Susan in "Love in Harness." After leaving Daly's her experience was varied. It included an extended engagement in prominent rôles with Modjeska on tour, an interval with Rosina Vokes, a season with Sol Smith Russell, rôles in "The Passing Show" at the Casino, "The Sorrows of Satan" at the Broadway, "The Last Chapter" at the Garden, "The Brixton Burglary" at the Herald Square, and in "Prince Otto" with Otis Skinner. Miss Filkins's last creations in New York, previous to her appearance as a star as Elisabeth Killigrew in "An American Widow" on September 6, 1909, were rôles in Charles Klein's three plays "The Daughters of Men," "The Stepsister," and "The Third Degree." In the last she was especially effective as the senior Mrs. Jeffries, and contributed her share to its excellent performance.

Mrs LESLIE CARTER

IN "THE UGLY DUCKLING"

MISS HELYETT

MRS. CARTER'S career is quite unique in stage annals. During the eighteen years of her stellar life in the theatre, from the time she made her first New York appearance, in 1890, until she made her first independent production in 1908, she played only six parts. During the latter portion of this period she was much admired in America as an actress of hysterically emotional rôles, and her fame was widely established. Her position was indeed such as no one before her has achieved and maintained without a much more extensive demonstration of versatility.

She was born Caroline Louise Dudley, and her parents were Kentuckians. Early in life she married Leslie Carter of Chicago. After eight years he secured a divorce, but she retained her former husband's name. Her early efforts were obscure and without significance except to David Belasco, who, in 1887, took her under his tutelage. Three years of obscurity followed, and in 1890 he announced her immediately as a star. On November 10 of that year she appeared as Kate Graydon in Paul Potter's drama, "The Ugly Duckling." Another year of obscurity followed this failure.

The next time Mrs. Carter appeared it was in a musical play from the French, "Miss Helyett," and, though only indifferently effective, she was kept on tour for two years. After two additional years of eclipse she once more emerged into public view, still a Belasco protégé, and was seen as Maryland Calvert in Mr. Belasco's "The Heart of Maryland." The principal scene was founded on the main incident in the poem "Curfew Shall Not Ring Tonight," and Mrs. Carter, as the heroine, who was supposed to swing out of the belfry on the bell's clapper, at last drew crowded houses.

Zaza was her next effort. She acted it first in 1898, and in this rôle she gave definite evidence of a gifted and polished technique in emotional acting. On this note she has based her succeeding efforts, which have numbered Belasco's own "Du Barry" in 1901; John Luther Long's "Adrea" in 1905, after which she and Belasco parted company; and since, under her own auspices, in Mr. Long's "Kassa" and "Vashti Herne," and in an occasional performance of Camille.

VASHTI HERNE

ZAZA

DU BARRY

IN "THE HEART OF MARYLAND"

AT WEBER AND FIELDS'S

IN "THE MUSIC MASTER"

IN "THE AUCTIONEER"

MR. DAVID WARFIELD

IN "A GRAND ARMY MAN"

THE most popular actor on the stage to-day is David Warfield. He has acted only three parts as a star and in each of these the dramatist has charged his character with all possible sympathy, but in every instance he has created and embellished with a consummate art which stamps him as a generic creator of the first rank.

He earned his first money in the theatre, but as an usher, at the Bush Street Theatre, in his native city of San Francisco. His début on the stage was made as Melter Moss, the Jew, in "A Ticket of Leave Man," at Napa, California. After one week he resumed ushering. His gifts as a mimic developed early and he grew into favor with clubs and lodges, to which he gave his services gratis. Finally he decided to try his fortunes in New York. With the assistance of some friends he got up a benefit for himself at Dashaway Hall, and the one hundred dollars that came in paid his way across the continent.

His first opportunity in New York was in an Eighth Avenue concert hall at fifteen dollars a week, and his specialty was the beginning of that Yiddish character which afterwards made him celebrated. Short experiences on tour followed, as a jay in "The Inspector," an Irishwoman in "O'Dowd's Neighbors," the Jew in "The City Directory," and as the country boy in "The Nutmeg Match."

His versatility began to tell and he became a member of the Casino company in 1894, and since then his career has been carefully watched. At the Casino he was one of the principal comedians for five years and there gave his first matured sketch of Simon Levi. In 1899 he joined Weber and Fields's company at their music hall, and his impersonations and burlesques while there were among the finest conceivable fun of their kind.

His Simon Levi, the Yiddish Eastsider, had grown into a characterization of national reputation and it was placed in a play called "The Auctioneer," by Charles Klein and Lee Arthur, which David Belasco presented at the Bijou Theatre, in September, 1901, with Mr. Warfield as a star. The quaint genre study grew in finesse by its transposition from the burlesque to the dramatic stage.

In 1904 Mr. Warfield astonished his admirers by a creation on a higher plane, and as different from the peddler as it were possible to conceive, his Anton von Barwig in Charles Klein's "The Music Master." This performance accented his versatility and confirmed his title to the vast popularity he had won. He appeared as Wes Bigelow, the Hoosier stage driver, in "A Grand Army Man," by the Misses Phelps and Short, in October, 1907.

MR. DAVID WARFIELD

MISS JULIE OPP

IN "THE BARBER OF NEW ORLEANS"

IN "A ROYAL RIVAL"

IN "HEROD"

SARAH BERNHARDT'S persuasion induced Julie Opp to become an actress after George Du Maurier's had failed. Miss Opp is a New York girl and she received her schooling in a convent in her native city. In 1895 she was visiting in London with a party of school girls, under the chaperonage of Kate Jordan, at the time that "Trilby" was the dramatic vogue, and one day at a girls' party she met George Du Maurier. He assured her she would make an ideal Trilby. The suggestion was not acted upon, but it bore fruit.

When she returned home Bernhardt was playing "Izeyll" at the Garden Theatre. Chartran also was in this country painting the portraits of celebrated people. Miss Opp met him and he presented her to the great French actress. The introduction took place at a rehearsal and the impulsive Frenchwoman at once stopped her actors to hear the American girl recite. "You have the youth and beauty of a Greek statue come to life," she said, and advised her to take up the career of the stage, but to begin in Europe. Miss Opp had already made an appreciable beginning as a writer for the magazines, but soon she abandoned that work and went to London. Her first appearance on the stage was made in that city at the Comedy Theatre and, curiously, in Bernhardt's company. The play was "Camille." Miss Opp was an extra woman in the ball-room scene. Bernhardt generously had a few lines written in for her which she was too frightened, however, to speak.

She acted with George Alexander and Julia Neilson, and less than two years after her début she made such a success as Mrs. Ware in "The Princess and the Butterfly" that she was brought across the ocean to play that rôle when the play was acted in New York. She went again to the St. James Theatre, London, in 1900, and was the originator of leading parts there for more than a year. She came home to create rôles in "A Royal Rival" and "Prince Charlie"; returned to London to play Katherine in "If I Were King," and since then she has acted the leading woman rôles continuously in support of her husband, William Faversham, achieving distinction by her plastic grace and forceful eloquence as Queen Marianne in Stephen Phillips's "Herod." Miss Opp has written much.

MISS JULIE OPP

MERCEDES IN "THE WORLD AND HIS WIFE"

MISS ELSIE JANIS

ELSIE JANIS is a winsome young star who has brought the freshness and charm of natural girlhood into the artificial soubrettedom of musical comedy. To a frank and ingratiating personality which at once establishes a bond of sympathy between herself and her audience, she adds a really remarkable gift for the mimicry of other actresses and actors.

Miss Janis exhibited her talents when a mere child in her native town of Columbus, Ohio, and was a great favorite with the Rev. Washington Gladden, pastor of her parents' church, and with William McKinley when he was Governor of the State. While Mr. McKinley was President, and she was with her parents in Washington, he invited her, then in her eleventh year, to entertain a large company of United States officials and Foreign representatives at the White House. Her success on this occasion was the subject of wide newspaper publicity and attracted New York theatrical managers to her. No one came forward, however, with a part for the little girl in a production, and she went into vaudeville, where her songs and imitations quickly advanced her to a position among the leading favorites. When only fourteen years old Miss Janis became a star in musical comedy and went on tour in revivals of "The Belle of New York," "The Fortune Teller," and "The Little Duchess."

New York had seen her before 1905, but as is often the case with metropolitan audiences, they look without seeing, and during that summer her imitations given at the New York Theatre Roof Garden were the most talked of entertainments of the town. A stellar appearance on Broadway in a musical comedy was at once arranged and her girlish personality and new imitations were a genuine success for "The Vanderbilt Cup." In 1907 she appeared in "The Hoyden" and in 1909 in "The Fair Co-Ed."

MISS ELSIE JANIS

IN "THE HOYDEN"

IN "THE FAIR CO-ED"

IN "THE VANDERBILT CUP"
Photograph by Hall

SHERLOCK HOLMES

Mr. WILLIAM GILLETTE

SHERLOCK HOLMES

IN "THE ADMIRABLE CRICHTON"

SHERLOCK HOLMES

WILLIAM GILLETTE has, a little unconsciously perhaps, given the note of leisure to his career because he has presented himself to the public only at intervals and because a cool self-possession and unhurried deliberation have distinguished most of his rôles. His characters may have reflected the man in a measure, but the catalogue of his achievements as actor and playwright denotes an active life.

Mr. Gillette was born in Hartford, Connecticut, in 1856. The stage attracted him from boyhood. When twenty years old he decided to adopt the theatre as a career and secured the position of utility man with the Ben de Bar stock company in New Orleans. His salary was nothing a week and a suggestion that it be raised resulted in his discharge. Mark Twain, who was a neighbor of his family, in Hartford, secured him a position at the Boston Theatre and he acted there and at the Boston Museum for two years. His New York début was made as the Prosecuting Attorney in "The Gilded Cage," in support of John T. Raymond at the New Park Theatre, April 29, 1877. Experience in Cincinnati and St. Louis stock companies followed.

Already he had begun to write plays and when he returned from the West to New York it was to act the title rôle in his comedy, "The Professor." The play enjoyed a run of nearly a year at the Madison Square Theatre. His next new rôle was Douglas Winthrop in Bronson Howard's "Young Mrs. Winthrop," in which he made a long tour, but meantime he assisted Mrs. Burnett with "Esmeralda," and made an adaptation from the German which was later merged with the English adaptation from the same source and achieved a large popularity as "The Private Secretary." He acted the Secretary for two years. His subsequent plays were "Held By the Enemy," "A Legal Wreck," "All the Comforts of Home" from the German, "Mr. Wilkinson's Widows," a dramatization of Rider Haggard's "She," "Ninety Days," "Because She Loved Him So" and "Settled Out of Court" from the French; and "Too Much Johnson." He acted Bean, the war correspondent, in the first of these and Billings in the last.

His greatest success was attained with his "Secret Service," in which he acted Lewis Dumont, first at the Broad Street Theatre, Philadelphia, May 15, 1895. His later appearances have been as the celebrated detective in his adaptation of Conan Doyle's "Sherlock Holmes," Mr. Crichton in Barrie's "The Admirable Crichton," and Dr. Carrington in his own "Clarice." Mr. Gillette wrote a second play in which the much admired Sherlock Holmes appeared. It was in one act and was called "The Painful Predicament of Sherlock Holmes." He and Miss Ethel Barrymore acted it in 1905 at a benefit in the Metropolitan Opera House.

Mr. WILLIAM GILLETTE

DR. CARRINGTON IN "CLARICE" — LEWIS DUMONT IN "SECRET SERVICE" — SAMSON

Miss Anna Held

ANNA HELD has been a prominent figure on the American stage as a singing comedienne ever since her first appearance at the Herald Square Theatre in September, 1896, when she sang "Oh Won't You Come and Play Wiz Me" in a revival of "A Parlor Match." Her manager-husband has since identified her in songs, costumes and type of humor with what is supposed to be most characteristically Parisian.

In spite of a German name Anna Held is the daughter of a Parisian father and a Parisian mother, and was born in Paris and lived there until she was twelve years old. Her account of her youth is sincerely pathetic. Her father was a manufacturer of gloves in a small way. Business vanished and he opened a restaurant. This, too, failed, and the girl spent part of her days in school and the rest earning a few sous curling plumes at first, then making button-holes, and finally sewing bits of fur together for caps. When she reached her twelfth year her father died. Her mother took her to London in search of relatives whom she did not find. They had a room next the Princess Theatre, and one day on the street her pretty face attracted the manager's attention and he gave her a place in the chorus. Ten months after they reached London her mother died.

Soon she was singing chansonettes in French, German, Polish and Spanish in the music halls of Holland, Sweden and Germany. At sixteen she reached Paris and sang at La Scala and El Dorado; thence she went to the Palace Music Hall, London, where she made a hit with the song which first made her popular in America, a translation from a German song, *Die Kleine Schrecke* (The Little Teazer). Florence Zeigfield was in the audience one evening and engaged her to come to America.

The rest is better known, for Miss Held has passed from one success to another as the last fourteen years have slipped by. Her performance in "The Parlor Match" was followed by her appearance as a star in "La Poupée," "The Little Duchess," and "Mlle. Napoleon." She spent the winter of 1904 with Weber and Fields at their Broadway Music Hall, and was absent from the stage throughout the year following. Since she has returned to the stage her pieces have been "A Parisian Model" and "Miss Innocence."

"A PARISIAN MODEL"

"THE LITTLE DUCHESS"

"MISS INNOCENCE"

"MLLE. NAPOLEON"

"PAPA'S WIFE"

MISS ANNA HELD

"MLLE. NAPOLEON"

"THE LITTLE DUCHESS"

MR. ROBERT "MANTELL"
KING RICHARD III RICHELIEU KING LEAR
Photographs by Hall

ROBERT MANTELL shares with E. H. Sothern and Louis James the distinction of a place in the front rank of those American players of to-day who devote themselves almost exclusively to the plays of Shakespeare. Mr. Mantell is Scotch by birth and parentage. The stage called him early in life and when his parents refused to hear of his becoming an actor he ran away from home before he was twenty and crossed the Atlantic to America. But he found no encouragement and after two weeks returned to England, where he made his first appearance at Rockdale, Lancashire, in 1876, under the name of R. Hudson. George Clarke, afterwards a leading player at Daly's, New York, was starring through England at that time in "The Shaughraun" and the young actor's second appearance was made with Mr. Clarke as Father Nolan in this play. Samuel Phelps found him in a provincial stock company shortly after this and took him to Sadler's Wells Theatre, London, where he had a valuable Shakespearian experience. After a brief tour in support of Marie de Grey in Shakespearian parts he made his second trip to America in 1878. On his return Mr. Mantell acted first in Helena Modjeska's company, but his stay was brief. After only a single season he returned to England to appear with George S. Knight in "Otto" and subsequently he supported Miss Wallis there in an extended standard repertoire.

His first appearance in New York was made at the Windsor Theatre in "The World" in 1882, and his second and more successful appeal for popularity was his Jack Herne in "The Romany Rye" at Booth's. The next year brought the production of "Fedora," by Fanny Davenport, and Mantell as Loris Ipanoff achieved a triumph which echoed for many years. In 1884 he created the leading part in "Called Back" at the Fifth Avenue, and in "Dakolar" at the Lyceum.

His finely developed ability and the popularity he achieved in all these rôles led to his début as a star at the Fifth Avenue in 1886 in "Tangled Lives." This was completely overshadowed by "Monbars" in which he next achieved a success equal to that of his Ipanoff in "Fedora." Mr. Mantell worked through long tours in various new and old plays and gradually built up a repertoire of classic and Shakespearian rôles. Since 1890 he has played "The Corsican Brothers," "The Marble Heart," "The Louisianian," "The Face in the Moonlight," "Parrhasius," "A Cavalier of France," "The Dagger and the Cross," "The Veiled Picture," both Othello and Iago in "Othello," Claude Melnotte in "The Lady of Lyons," "Richard III," "Romeo and Juliet," "King Lear," "Macbeth," "The Merchant of Venice," "Julius Caesar," "Richelieu" and "King John."

KING JOHN

LOUIS XI

MR. ROBERT MANTELL
Photograph by Hall

MACBETH

KING LEAR

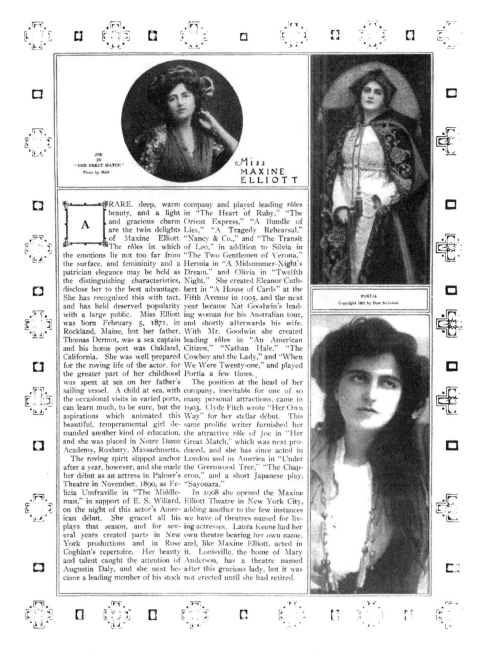

JOE
IN
"HER GREAT MATCH"
Photo by Hall

Miss MAXINE ELLIOTT

PORTIA
Copyright 1901 by Burr McIntosh

A RARE, deep, warm beauty, and a light and gracious charm are the twin delights of Maxine Elliott. The rôles in which the emotions lie not too far from the surface, and femininity and a patrician elegance may be held as the distinguishing characteristics, disclose her to the best advantage. She has recognized this with tact, and has held deserved popularity with a large public. Miss Elliott was born February 5, 1871, in Rockland, Maine, but her father, Thomas Dermot, was a sea captain and his home port was Oakland, California. She was well prepared for the roving life of the actor, for the greater part of her childhood was spent at sea on her father's sailing vessel. A child at sea, with the occasional visits in varied ports, can learn much, to be sure, but the aspirations which animated this beautiful, temperamental girl demanded another kind of education, and she was placed in Notre Dame Academy, Roxbury, Massachusetts.

The roving spirit slipped anchor after a year, however, and she made her début as an actress in Palmer's Theatre in November, 1890, as Felicia Umfraville in "The Middleman," in support of E. S. Willard, on the night of this actor's American début. She graced all his plays that season, and for several years created parts in New York productions and in Rose Coghlan's repertoire. Her beauty and talent caught the attention of Augustin Daly, and she next became a leading member of his stock company and played leading rôles in "The Heart of Ruby," "The Orient Express," "A Bundle of Lies," "A Tragedy Rehearsal," "Nancy & Co.," and "The Transit of Leo," in addition to Silvia in "The Two Gentlemen of Verona," Hermia in "A Midsummer-Night's Dream," and Olivia in "Twelfth Night." She created Eleanor Cuthbert in "A House of Cards" at the Fifth Avenue in 1905, and the next year became Nat Goodwin's leading woman for his Australian tour, and shortly afterwards his wife. With Mr. Goodwin she created leading rôles in "An American Citizen," "Nathan Hale," "The Cowboy and the Lady," and "When We Were Twenty-one," and played Portia a few times.

The position at the head of her own company, inevitable for one of so many personal attractions, came in 1903. Clyde Fitch wrote "Her Own Way" for her stellar début. This same prolific writer furnished her the attractive rôle of Joe in "Her Great Match," which was next produced, and she has since acted in London and in America in "Under the Greenwood Tree," "The Chaperon," and a short Japanese play, "Sayonara."

In 1908 she opened the Maxine Elliott Theatre in New York City, adding another to the few instances we have of theatres named for living actresses. Laura Keene had her own theatre bearing her own name, and, like Maxine Elliott, acted in it. Louisville, the home of Mary Anderson, has a theatre named after this gracious lady, but it was not erected until she had retired.

IN "WHEN WE WERE TWENTY-ONE"

IN "THE TWO GENTLEMEN OF VERONA"

Miss
MAXINE ELLIOTT

IN "IF I WERE KING"

PETER PAN

IN "THE SERIO-COMIC GOVERNESS"

IN "RICHARD LOVELACE"

Miss CECILIA LOFTUS

CECILIA LOFTUS first made herself known to American amusement seekers as an exceptionally able mimic. In those days she was "Cissie" Loftus. The vaudeville stage claimed her all for its own. Her vogue was remarkable, and her imitations of Bernhardt, May Irwin, and other as markedly contrasted stage celebrities were considered as faithful as it was possible to make them.

Miss Loftus is the daughter of Marie Loftus, one of England's most popular music hall singers. She was born in Glasgow in 1876, and when only fifteen she was taken from school and gave imitations and sang original songs at the head of the bill at the Oxford Music Hall, London. She played her first part, Haidee, in one of the Gaiety Theatre's musical comedies, in October, 1893. In 1894 she came to America and at once achieved an enormous success as a mimic. When she returned to England she spent four years in the music halls, except for a single engagement as the Goose Girl with Martin Harvey in "The Children of the King," at the Court Theatre.

She had, however, determined to make a place for herself among the actresses of her time. To this end she returned to America and engaged herself to support Madame Modjeska, and as a member of her company appeared at the Fifth Avenue Theatre during March, 1900, as Leonie in "The Ladies' Battle," Viola in "Twelfth Night," and Hero in "Much Ado About Nothing." These performances established her as an actress, and she played conspicuous rôles in "A Man of Forty" and "Lady Huntsworth's Experiment," at Daly's; Lady Mildred in "The Slaves of Night," at the Broadway; and, as leading woman for E. H. Sothern, Lucy Sacheverell in "Richard Lovelace," Katherine in "If I Were King," and, later, Ophelia in "Hamlet" and Perpetua in "The Proud Prince." She acted Marguerite in "Faust," and both Nerissa and Jessica in "The Merchant of Venice" with Henry Irving at the Lyceum Theatre, London, in 1902.

Daniel Frohman advanced Miss Loftus as a star at the New Lyceum Theatre in September, 1904, when she played Eileen O'Keefe in Zangwill's comedy, "The Serio-Comic Governess." She was the "Peter Pan" of Barrie's play during its Christmas revival in London in 1905. Since that time Miss Loftus has devoted her public appearances to vaudeville again, except for an engagement in the Weber Theatre company in "Dream City."

MISS CECILIA LOFTUS

MR. HENRY E. DIXEY

TO some actors it is given to make such an overwhelming hit at one point in their careers that they are able to live it down only after long and persistent demonstrations of their versatility. Henry E. Dixey made such a hit in a burlesque called "Adonis." It was produced first at the Bijou Theatre September 4, 1884, and it had a record run of 603 nights at this theatre and many months in London. He played it for nearly five consecutive years. He became less well known to the public by his own name than as "Adonis Dixey." This rôle became not only the measure but the pattern of what managers and audiences expected of him as long as they remembered it. Yet it was no gauge of Dixey's ability as an actor, as he has proved many times since in pieces which failed of the wonderful success attained by "Adonis." One of its well remembered features was his imitation of Henry Irving, then making his earliest visit to America.

Mr. Dixey made his first appearance on the stage at the Howard Athenæum in Boston, the city in which he was born, in 1859. He was but nine years old at the time and he acted Peanuts in Augustin Daly's play "Under the Gaslight." He was in Rice's celebrated company which, in 1875, first presented "Evangeline," playing the forelegs of the celebrated heifer of which Richard Golden was the hind legs. Before he left the company he had acted nearly every male part.

For several years he was the favorite comedian in the American productions of the Gilbert and Sullivan and other light operas, giving always a grace, delicacy, and humor to his performances which audiences delighted in and have not been treated to since. After the Adonis interval his conspicuous appearances were in "The Seven Ages," "The Solicitor," "The Man of a Hundred Heads," Bunthorne in "Patience," "The Sorcerer," and during two seasons in leading light comedy parts at Daly's Theatre. From 1896 to 1905 he played sometimes in musical pieces and sometimes in vaudeville, but in the latter year he obtained substantial favor as Lieutenant Robert Warburton a star in "The Man on the Box, and during the winter of 1908 he appeared as Pa in "Mary Jane's Pa

MR. HENRY E. DIXEY ADONIS From Theatre Magazine

IN "MARY JANE'S PA"

DAVID GARRICK

IN "MISTRESS NELL."
Copyright by A. Dupont

Miss HENRIETTA CROSMAN

HENRIETTA CROSMAN'S father was a United States army officer and she was born at the Army post near Wheeling, W. Va. Her mother was a Miss Wick of Northern Ohio and a niece of Stephen C. Foster, who wrote "My Old Kentucky Home." Her childhood was spent wherever her father's stations took the family, from Dakota and Montana to Texas.

Rebuff, grit, perseverance, and good cheer have won Miss Crosman her present position. Her parents' fortunes made self-support obvious and she went to Paris to study for grand opera. Illness cut that career. Returning home, she went on the stage, and her first part was Letty Lee in "The White Slave." After an itinerant interval as Parthenia and Virginia in support of Robert Downing, she came to New York and was soon a popular member of the Lyceum company. At this time she created rôles in the original casts of "The Idler," "Mr. Wilkinson's Widows," and "The Junior Partner."

Her first real taste of individual success came, however, in 1892 when she created the title part in "Gloriana," at Hermann's (later the Princess) Theatre. Her performance was the talk of the town, but, after three days, illness once more overtook her and she did not play again that season.

A fresh start was made the next year, and she acted all kinds of parts in stock companies in the far West and, under Augustin Daly and both Frohmans, in New York before she again made a really resounding hit. This was at the Bijou Theatre in October, 1900, as Nell Gwynne in George Hazleton's "Mistress Nell."

Since that time Miss Crosman has been a conspicuous star devoting herself to high comedy in modern, romantic and Shakespearian rôles. High spirits, sprightly humor and unflagging vivacity usually distinguish her acting. She has played Joan in "Joan of the Shoals," Rosalind in "As You Like It," Philippa in "The Sword of the King," Mistress Kitty in "Sweet Kitty Bellairs," "Nance Oldfield," "Madelaine," "Mary, Mary, Quite Contrary," Peggy O'Mara in "All-of-a-Sudden Peggy," Christian in "The Christian Pilgrim," which was a dramatization of Bunyan's "Pilgrim's Progress," and Catherine in "Sham."

MISS LULU GLASER

LULU GLASER skipped all the romantic hardships which lead from obscurity to prominence. She simply came and saw and conquered. Born in Allegheny City, Pennsylvania, on June 2, 1872, she studied in the public schools, and then decided to improve her voice and go on the stage. Others have planned the same plans, but for Miss Glaser there was quick and easy realization. She took vocal lessons until she felt that she had a voice to offer and went straight to New York. That was in 1891. Francis Wilson was then on the crest of his success as a comic opera star, and was appearing in "The Lion Tamer" at the Broadway Theatre. Miss Glaser entered the chorus. Her pretty face, vivacious manner and marked personality attracted Mr. Wilson, and he made her understudy for Marie Jansen. Miss Glaser got her opportunity as Angelina, and she has ever since been a popular singing comédienne.

She was Mr. Wilson's chief assistant for nine seasons and shared in all his successes. Her rôles included Lazuli in "The Merry Monarch," Javotte in the first revival of "Erminie," Elverine in "The Devil's Deputy," Rita in "The Chieftain," Pirette in "Half a King," Jacquelin in "The Little Corporal," and Roxane in the musical version of "Cyrano de Bergerac" produced in the autumn of 1899.

Her popularity had increased at this time to a point where it seemed practical to appear at the head of her own company. Her début as a star was made a year later as Anne in "Sweet Anne Page." This was followed by Angela in "The Prima Donna," not the same as Fritzi Scheff's; "Dolly Varden"; Mary Tudor in a musical version of Paul Kester's play "When Knighthood Was in Flower," and entitled, "The Madcap Princess"; Dorothy Gay in "Miss Dolly Dollars"; "Lola of Berlin"; and "One of the Boys." During 1908 she spent a short interval in Joseph Weber's musical burlesque company.

IN "THE BELLE OF BRITTANY"

Mr. FRANK DANIELS

FRANK DANIELS took up comic opera after a successful career in comedy without music and has held himself in a position at the front of the column of comedians who are genuinely and continuously funny. It is not quite fair to his many other methods of fun, but Mr. Daniels has become known as the comedian with the trick eyebrows. They are truly well trained and docile eyebrows, and when they go up they carry shouts of laughter with them. But he is quite as funny with his back turned to the audience, and to see the little comedian set his shoulders and stride majestically up stage provokes as loud a laugh as any line a librettist ever gave him.

Mr. Daniels was born in Dayton, Ohio, in 1860. His boyhood was spent in Boston where his family moved soon after the opening of the Civil War. There he attended school, and for three years was employed as a wood engraver. At the same time he studied singing at the New England Conservatory of Music. He went down to Salem for his stage début in 1879. The Opera was "The Chimes of Normandy." His rôle was the sheriff.

Engagements followed in various companies without particular success until he made a hit in a piece called "An Electric Doll," and he played with the company presenting this farce for three years in America and England. His next success came in 1884 as Old Sport in Hoyt's "A Rag Baby." The country laughed at Old Sport for three years. A still bigger hit was made next in "Little Puck." No one whose memory of stage favorites covers the seven years during which he starred in "Little Puck" has forgotten his Packington Giltedge.

Since then the list of comic operas in which he has starred includes "The Wizard of the Nile," "The Idol's Eye," "The Ameer," "Miss Simplicity," "The Office Boy," "Sergeant Brue," "The Tattooed Man," "Mr. Hook of Holland," and "The Belle of Brittany." It is useless to recall the parts he played, but the fun has been equally plentiful in his quaint, individual way.

Miss VIRGINIA HARNED

LADY URSULA

VIRGINIA HARNED has punctuated a long and ambitious career before the public with certain unmistakable successes which stamp her an able and versatile actress as well as a popular star. The first of these were her delightful comedy performances in support of E. H. Sothern in the old Lyceum days: her dramatic creation of Trilby O'Ferrall in "Trilby"; romantic, bubbling Ursula in "The Adventure of Lady Ursula"; and tearful, emotional "Iris." Many actresses have maintained a conspicuous position on a fraction of such varied excellence, yet Miss Harned has added to these a long series of other ambitious rôles, the latter ones showing the marked influence of her acquaintance with Pinero's protagonist.

Miss Harned had been playing on the New York stage less than five months when she joined Mr. Sothern's company at the Lyceum. Born in Boston in 1868, she was taken to England by her parents when a baby, and was educated there. She returned when sixteen and acted first on tour with a company playing "Our Boarding House," later in "A Night Off" and "A Still Alarm," and made her New York début at the Fourteenth Street Theatre in "A Long Lane," March 31, 1890. In the May following she appeared at Palmer's Theatre in "The Editor"; in June as Madge Ravenscroft in "Lara"; and August 26, as Clara Dexter, the leading woman rôle in "The Maister of Woodbarrow" at the Lyceum. Mr. Sothern was the star in this play, and he and Miss Harned were married later and often acted together. Clara Dexter was followed by a series of her most admired performances: Drusilla Ives in "The Dancing Girl," Fanny Hadden in "Captain Lettarblair," Mrs. Sylvester in "The New Woman," and in several plays under A. M. Palmer's management.

When this celebrated manager produced Paul Potter's dramatization of George Du Maurier's "Trilby" at the Garden Theatre, April 15, 1895, Miss Harned made a great success as the hypnotized heroine. Except for a brief interval in Sardou's "Spiritism," she spent the next five years in E. H. Sothern's company, playing the leading-woman parts in "An Enemy to the King," "'Change Alley," "The Lady of Lyons," "The Adventure of Lady Ursula," "A Colonial Girl," "The Song of the Sword," and "The King's Musketeers"; Rautendelein in "The Sunken Bell" and Ophelia in "Hamlet."

Since 1901 Miss Harned has starred alone. Her principal productions have been "Alice of Old Vincennes," a dramatization of Maurice Thompson's novel by Edward Rose, "Iris," "The Lady Shore," "The Light That Lies in Woman's Eyes," by Mr. Sothern, "Camille," "The Love Letter," and "Anna Karenina." She later appeared in vaudeville in "The Idol of the Hour" of her own writing.

OPHELIA

Miss VIRGINIA HARNED

MR.
WALKER
WHITESIDE

HAMLET
Copyright 1896 by B. J. Falk

SHYLOCK
Copyright 1896 by B. J. Falk

IN "ROBERT OF SICILY"

WALKER WHITESIDE began his stage experience as a "boy tragedian." He was born in Logansport, Indiana, and attended school in Chicago. He came under the direction of Samuel Kayser, the founder of the Chicago Conservatory, and after two years' study and instruction he made his début as a Shakespearian star, a position from which he has not receded during more than twenty years on the stage.

He came into New York an absolute stranger in 1893 and appeared in "Hamlet" at the Union Square Theatre. A repetition of the James Owen O'Connor and Count Johannes "eggs and vegetables" nights was anticipated by those in the audience the first night and prepared for by many. Instead the audience heard him with surprise, then wonder, and finally enthusiastic applause. The critics proclaimed a "Hamlet" of quality and astonishing in one so young. The theatre was crowded before the first week closed.

With the prestige of the approval of New York he resumed his tour, but for fifteen years he seldom played even in cities accustomed to support actors for one week. His repertoire embraced Hamlet, Shylock, Richard III, Othello and King Lear. When Shakespeare failed him, he took up romantic plays, many of which he wrote himself, and in the cities which he visited season after season he is well remembered in dramatizations of Stanley Weyman's "The Man in Black" and "The Red Cockade," and in Paul and Vaughan Kester's "Cousin to the King," "We Are King," "Heart and Sword." Paul Kester's version of "Eugene Aram," "David Garrick's Love" and "The Magic Melody."

In 1908 Mr. Whiteside entered into an alliance with Liebler & Co. and at once appeared in W. J. Locke's "The Beloved Vagabond." The play lacked popular elements, but his performance of the title rôle was a work of real beauty and his David Quixano in Zangwill's "The Melting Pot" has established him in the place to which his seasoned art entitles him among players of metropolitan prestige.

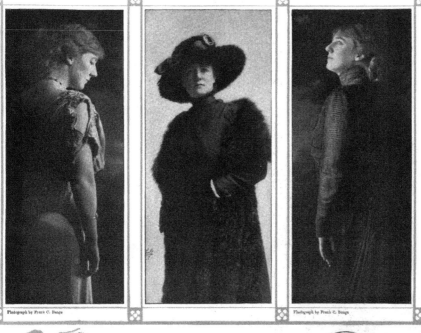

 MISS NANCE O'NEIL

N ANCE O'NEIL is an actress whose endeavors have been projected on a high plane, and she has repeatedly been accorded enthusiastic praise by the best informed and most discriminating critics. She has been pronounced a tragic actress of real genius, yet she has been absent almost continuously from those stages where an artist of her endowment belongs.

Miss O'Neil was born in Oakland, California, and received her training for the stage from McKee Rankin, under whose direction she has appeared almost continuously until recently. She made her début in a play called "Sarah" at the Alcazar Theatre, San Francisco. The career thus entered upon has been pursued for years in all parts of the globe, in comedy and in tragedy, in stock companies and as a star, in the standard rôles which have tested great artists of many generations, and in creations which have stamped her an artist with original as well as traditional ideas. Pervading her whole association with the stage is the strong note of deep, rich resources and lofty ideals worked out zealously, continuously.

Since she has been proclaimed in all the great parts she has played her repertoire may indeed be her laurel, for she has acted Lady Macbeth, Rosalind, Juliet, Leah, Magda, Viola, Nancy Sykes, Camille, Lady Isabel, Fedora, Trilby, Parthenia, Meg Merillies, La Tosca, Lady Teazle, Judith, Queen Elizabeth, Tess of the d'Urbervilles, Hedda Gabler, Marie in "The Fires of St. John," Rebecca West in "Rosmersholm," Zoraya in "The Sorceress," Monna Vanna, Agnes and Cleo. In the winter of 1909 she came under the management of David Belasco, and created in English the rôle of Odette de Maiguy in the translation of Wolff and Le Roux's "The Lily," which was acted at the Vaudeville Theatre in Paris by Suzanne Desprès.

IN "THE ROSE OF THE RANCHO"

Miss FRANCES STARR

FRANCES STARR has been on the stage less than ten years, of which she has been a star for three. So much of this time has been spent in New York that to the country at large she is a mere name. Her sudden success is looked upon as one of the fairy devices of the stage fates. It was prepared for, however, by a long schooling in various stock companies where she acted hundreds of parts.

Miss Starr was born in Oneonta, New York, but when very young her family moved to Albany and there she grew up and went to school. That city has supported an energetic and carefully recruited stock company for many summers and in 1900 Miss Starr made her début with one of these organizations and played a few of the minor parts. In the autumn of that year she joined Henry V. Donnelly's stock company at the Murray Hill Theatre, New York City. During three consecutive years she acted a new part on an average of once a week, beginning with bits and eventually playing the leading ingenue rôles. In 1903 she crossed the continent and acted thirty-three parts in thirty-seven weeks with the Alcazar Stock Company, of San Francisco, and returned to the Atlantic Seaboard for a further service in stock at the Castle Square Theatre in Boston for one year and during a few weeks of the autumn of 1905 with the Proctor Company of Fifth Avenue Theatre.

Charles Richman was at the time playing a special engagement at the Fifth Avenue Theatre. When he left to appear in "Gallops" a few blocks further uptown at the Garrick Theatre he took Miss Starr with him and gave her her opportunity to create a part in a New York production. From that discovery dates her rise. David Belasco, in May, 1906, engaged her to play the leading ingenue with David Warfield in "The Music Master," and under his patronage and with the opportunities he has given her Miss Starr has become one of the best known and admired of the younger actresses in America.

None of her efforts had attracted the public's attention before she made her first appearance as Juanita in "The Rose of the Rancho" at the Belasco in the autumn of 1906, and her delightful performance was a thorough surprise. But she proved that it was no accident by her equal expertness as Laura Murdock in "The Easiest Way," a part entirely dissimilar to Juanita.

IN "THE EASIEST WAY"

Miss Frances Starr

RICHARD BREWSTER IN "THE THIRD DEGREE"

BLACK EAGLE IN "STRONGHEART"

JOHN BURKETT RYDER IN "THE LION AND THE MOUSE"

MR. EDMUND BREESE

EDMUND BREESE learned his profession in the hardest of all schools — the road. Much is said of the relentless work of a stock company, where there is a new part to learn every week. In that there is at least a variety of roles, and it is founded on domestic permanence and the elimination of travel. But Breese for fourteen years just traveled, traveled, traveled. He seldom saw New York and never played there. Most of the tours during this space were made up of perpetual moves from town to town with only an occasional stop in a two or three night stand or, at rare intervals, for the restful length of a week. But in all his road associations the standard of the plays was high, he acted with superior players and there was an absence of relaxed endeavor which comes with a long run in cities. On tour nearly every night is a first night.

Though Mr. Breese was born in Brooklyn he made his first appearance on the stage in the West in 1892, at the age of twenty-two. After four rough years he was engaged to play the heavy parts in the support of Mlle. Hortense Rhéa, a French actress of rare gifts who won wide popularity throughout America during long tours here. He became James O'Neill's leading man in 1898 and the association was a long one. With Mlle. Rhéa he played Napoleon in "The Empress Josephine," Leicester in "Mary Stuart," Sartorys in "Frou Frou," Benedick in "Much Ado About Nothing," Shylock in "The Merchant of Venice," and Lord Jeffrys in Paul Kester's "Nell Gwynne." With Mr. O'Neill he acted Appius in "Virginius," Nortier in "Monte Cristo," and Rochefort in "The Musketeers."

The last-named production brought him his first appearance in New York City. He was not through with his travels, however, until he appeared at the Hudson Theatre with Robert Edeson in "Strongheart," in January, 1905, playing Buckley, the trainer, and Black Eagle, the Indian Chief. New York has held him almost continuously since. There was an end of what the touring actor calls "living in his trunk." At the same theatre in 1906 Mr. Breese created John Burkett Ryder in Charles Klein's "The Lion and the Mouse" and played it there for two seasons continuously and, in 1908, he created Richard Brewster, the attorney, in the same author's "The Third Degree," which also had a run of more than a year in the Hudson Theatre. Between the last two plays he appeared in London in "Strongheart" with Mr. Edeson and in a special production of "The Lion and the Mouse."

IN "IT HAPPENED IN NORDLAND"

IN "MARRYING MARY"
Photograph by Frank C. Bangs

IN "NANCY BROWN"

MISS MARIE CAHILL

IN "THE BOYS AND BETTY"
Photograph by Frank C. Bangs

SINGING comediennes are rare. There have been three conspicuous examples, in the last decade, of women who could interpret a song as they could a character, with an unerring sense of humor and a contagious personality, with a gift for pointing the fun delicately yet crisply; Fay Templeton, May Irwin, and Marie Cahill.

Miss Cahill is a Brooklyn girl and made her first essays on the stage in neighborhood stock companies. After a début in New York in "C. O. D.," she went into Charles Hoyt's "A Tin Soldier," and then "Superba" and "Excelsior, Jr." Miss Cahill played, during the season of 1896, in London in "Morocco Bound." During the six years following she appeared in leading parts in "Sporting Life," "The Runaway Girl," at Daly's; "Three Little Lambs," at the Fifth Avenue; "Star and Garter," at the Victoria; "The Wild Rose," at the Knickerbocker; and "Sally in Our Alley," at the Broadway.

With singers of popular songs it is sometimes the song, as well as the play in which it is sung, that becomes identified with them. Miss Cahill interpolated in "The Wild Rose" a song which quite eclipsed the piece, survived through the life of her next comedy, and finally gave its name to the comedy in which she made her first appearance as a star. This was the memorable "Nancy Brown." Another song which she made popular was "Under the Bamboo Tree."

Miss Cahill has acted at the head of her own company in "Nancy Brown" in 1903, spent the winter of 1904 at Lew Fields's (later the Hackett) Theatre in "It Happened in Nordland," and she has since starred as Molly Moonshine in "Moonshine," as Mary Montgomery in "Marrying Mary," which was Edwin Milton Royle's farce "My Wife's Husbands" with few alterations, and as Betty Barbeau in "The Boys and Betty."

IN "THE ROYAL FAMILY"

MISS ANNIE RUSSELL

ONE of the most gifted actresses of sympathetic rôles and one of the most beloved players of her generation is Annie Russell. She came into prominence when a very young girl and has revealed a long gallery of winsome characters, sometimes poetic, sometimes romantic and sometimes realistic, but all outlined with delicate art.

Miss Russell is another of our players who has grown out of a stage childhood in a juvenile Pinafore company. Her first years covered long distances. She was born in Liverpool, was taken to Canada when a child and made her début with Rose Eytinge as Jeanne in "Miss Moulton," at Montreal, and then traveled with a juvenile opera company through the United States, West Indies and South America.

These experiences may have counted in the formation of her character and work, but she was inconspicuous until she created "Esmeralda" in Mrs. Frances Hodgson Burnett's play of that name at Madison Square Theatre in 1881. She remained at this theatre for eight years, when illness obliged her to retire.

Miss Russell returned to the stage in 1894 and played in "The New Woman," "Keeping Up," and "Lethe," and with Nat Goodwin in "Ambition," "In Mizzouri," "A Gilded Fool" and "David Garrick." In September, 1896, in the theatre of her great success as Esmeralda, she made an even greater triumph in "Sue," a play founded on Bret Harte's story of the same name. During the next two years she created Betty Fondacre in "The Mysterious Mr. Bugle," Ann May in "The Salt of the Earth," Madge in "Dangerfield, '95," Margaret in "The Scenario," and Sylvia in "A Bachelor's Romance," and delighted London with her "Sue."

On her return home she took her place among the stars and presented the series of characters in which she is best known to the present generation of theatre goers: "Catherine," Jerome's "Miss Hobbs," Princess Angela in "The Royal Family," Winifred Stanton in Fitch's "The Girl and the Judge," Peggy in "Mice and Men," Jacqueline in "The Younger Mrs. Parling," Genevieve in "Brother Jacques," Jinny in Zangwill's play "Jinny the Carrier," in London; Barbara in Bernard Shaw's "Major Barbara," Hannah Lightfoot in Paul Kester's "Friend Hannah," Puck in "A Midsummer-Night's Dream" with which she opened the Astor Theatre and Mary in "The Stronger Sex." During the winter of 1906 Miss Russell became a member of the company at The New Theatre.

MAJOR BARBARA
Miss ANNIE RUSSELL
Copyright by Ernest K. Mills

MR. GEORGE COHAN

IN "THE YANKEE PRINCE"

GEORGE WASHINGTON, JR.

G EORGE M. COHAN is the originator of the Cohan dance, the Cohan corner-of-the-mouth curtain speech, the Cohan brand of musical comedy entertainment, the Cohan model for Elsie Janis's popular imitations and, though Nature collaborated efficiently, of Cohan's Royal Family. His audiences know him for a busy personality—when as a playwright he dramatizes himself and as a manager puts himself forward as a star in the musical comedies which as a dramatist and composer he writes himself. His other activities off the stage confirm this impression.

Mr. Cohan was born in Providence, Rhode Island, July 4, 1878, and his stage début was made as a violinist with a "Daniel Boone" company in Haverstraw, New York, when he was nine years old. The next season he traveled with his parents and his sister in a play by his father, "The Two Barneys," and soon thereafter he was seen as the historic Boy in a tour of Governor Peck's popular papers in Peck's Sun called "Peck's Bad Boy." Various experiences followed in stock companies and on the road, until his father, mother, sister Josephine and himself formed a quartette under the name of the Four Cohans and played snappy farces in vaudeville.

About this time George Cohan began to write songs, music and sketches for vaudeville and astonished everyone by the rapidity, versatility and enormity of his output. One of these he extended from one act to three acts with music and, as "The Governor's Son" it was the foundation of his extending reputation. This was followed by other extensions of his vaudeville skits and some wholly new pieces. For his own appearances he wrote "Running for Office," "Little Johnnie Jones," "George Washington, Jr." and "The Yankee Prince," in all of which he starred. He is also the author of "Forty-Five Minutes from Broadway," in which Fay Templeton sang "So Long, Mary," and made her last appearances before retiring; "Fifty Miles from Boston"; "The Honeymooners"; "The Talk of New York," which presented Victor Moore as a star; and a revision of his play "Popularity" with the addition of music, which he called "The Man Who Owns Broadway," for Raymond Hitchcock. Mr. Cohan not only writes the comedies, but he writes the lyrics and the music. He produces them and is a partner in other theatrical enterprises as well.

IN "GEORGE WASHINGTON, JR."

Miss Carlotta Nillson

THERE is the pathos of her own lonely North in Carlotta Nillson's struggle in life and the same aloofness is often borne by her marked individuality and unique methods into the impression she sends across the footlights.

Miss Nillson was born in Sweden and was half an orphan from birth, for when she was born her father had already died. Her mother brought her to America when she was still young and they followed the beaten path of their countrymen into Wisconsin and Minnesota. Necessity knocked on the door very early in life and she went into a family as companion to a group of rich children younger than herself. When she and her mother moved to San Francisco, Modjeska was playing there and she was given "walking parts."

New York seemed necessary to a successful beginning. When she reached there and presented a letter of introduction to Augustin Daly he gave her a place in the chorus of a musical comedy playing at his theatre. She gave this up to play a part in "The Private Secretary" on a long tour, from the

IN "THE THREE OF US"

fatigues of which she was plunged into an illness. Her next appearances were in "The Crust of Society" and "Shenandoah." After this she gave up the stage and lived in retirement in England. She studied all the while, however, and when she took up her career again while in England she played in "The Ambassador" and "The Happy Life."

The unsuccessful struggle with obscurity went on, lightened temporarily by engagements to play Eunice in "Quo Vadis?" and an adventuress in "Among Those Present" with Mrs. LeMoyne. The end of obscurity if not of struggle came finally and New York woke up to the presence of an unusual actress when Miss Nillson appeared as Mrs. Elvsted in "Hedda Gabler" with Mrs. Fiske at the Manhattan Theatre, in 1903. Her next appearance was in a special matinée of a play called "Love's Pilgrimage." The effect of her skilful work in this play came the following season when Charles Frohman engaged her to play Letty in Pinero's play of that name, with William Faversham. Her performance of Letty bore out the promise of Mrs. Elvsted. Her next revelations of her art were in "The Man on the Box," "The Three of Us," "This Woman and This Man," and "For Better or for Worse."

CAMILLE

Miss OLGA NETHERSOLE

SAPHO

CARMEN

OLGA NETHERSOLE is one of the many actresses whom England has sent to America in the full flower of their art. She is one of the few who have remained and completely identified herself with the theatrical experience of playgoers in all parts of this country. She first came to this side of the Atlantic in 1894 and since then her appearances elsewhere have been few.

The daughter of an English barrister and a Spanish mother, she was born in London and proved herself proficient in amateur theatricals when a young girl. Her first years on the stage were spent in English touring companies and she made her London début in 1888 in a production of "The Union Jack," at the Adelphi. She at once stepped into leading parts and when the Garrick Theatre was opened in 1889 she was given the rôle of Janet Preece to create in Pinero's "The Profligate." At this theatre she later played in "La Tosca" and "A Fool's Paradise." A ten months' tour in Australia was her next experience and when she returned to London she appeared as Zicka in a revival of "Diplomacy" and created leading parts in "The Silent Battle" and in "The Transgressor." The latter play was the vehicle of her first American appearance, October 15, 1894, at Palmer's Theatre. After her success here her appearances alternated between England and America. In England she succeeded Mrs. Patrick Campbell in "The Notorious Mrs. Ebbsmith," and produced in dramatic form "Carmen," in which she exploited the celebrated "Nethersole kiss"; "The Termagant," and Fitch's "Sapho."

In America Miss Nethersole played all these parts and to her repertoire she added revivals of "Camille," "Adrienne Lecouvreur," "Denise," "Romeo and Juliet," and "The Second Mrs. Tanqueray." Among the plays of which she has made the first production here are "The Labyrinth," "The Awakening," William J. Hurlbut's "The Writing on the Wall," and Asa Steele's "Locke of Wall Street."

Beginning June 4, 1907, Miss Nethersole, during ten successive evenings, played in English ten different rôles from her repertoire at the Theatre Sarah Bernhardt, Paris. Her popularity throughout America is great, for she has often proved herself an emotional actress of wonderful charm, distinction, insight and power.

IN "I PAGLIACCI"

MISS OLGA NETHERSOLE

IN "THE LABYRINTH"

MR. LOUIS MANN

LOUIS MANN is an actor who has associated himself in the public mind with German character parts. His talents are really more comprehensive, but this is the type of part he has played with only a few exceptions since he became a prominent player; and as audiences are generally observers and rarely discerners, Louis Mann is known as an actor of German characters. As a matter of fact the first third of his career was devoted to classic rôles and straight light comedy.

Mr. Mann was born in New York City and made his début there, at the age of three and a half, in "Snow Flake," a pantomime founded on one of the Grimm Fairy Tales, at the old Stadt Theatre in the Bowery in 1868. At that time this theatre was the principal playhouse in the celebrated old street. His retirement was as precipitate as his début, and more nearly permanent, for he did not emerge into the public eye again until he was eighteen years old. In the interval his parents had moved to San Francisco, and he attended school there.

When Lawrence Barrett and John McCullough came to San Francisco in the early eighties, he haunted the theatre and finally was given small parts. He barnstormed his way eastward and through the East, often playing Hamlet. Later he had parts in "The Gladiator" and in "Othello" and other Shakespearian plays with Tommaso Salvini and Lewis Morrison and Marie Prescott.

One of the milestones in his early experience was his first opportunity to create a rôle in a new production in a New York theatre, which came to him in the part of Page in Oscar Wilde's first play, "Vera," at the Union Square in 1883. This occasion was not of large consequence to any one but himself, for his real demonstrations of talent were to come later. He played on long tours in "Called Back," "Lost," and other dramas, and his name appears in casts with E. H. Sothern and Cyril Maude, who later became celebrated as a London actor-manager. Mr. Maude's health broke down and he was sent across the Atlantic to the Rocky Mountains. While he was in the United States he joined Daniel Bandmann, who was starring in "Dr. Jekyll and Mr. Hyde." Louis Mann was another member of this company, and his performance of Gabriel Utterson gave him his first substantial success.

When "Incog," later turned into the musical comedy "Three Twins" with such success, was produced at the Bijou in 1892, Mr. Mann was one of the hits of the farce as Dick. He followed this with struggling tours in "The Laughing Girl" and "Hannah," reappeared in New York in "The Merry World" as Svengali and followed this with Herr Von Moser in "The Strange Adventures of Miss Brown," at the Standard in 1895, for which he was much praised. This committed him securely to German characters in New York. Subsequently he played in "The Girl From Paris," in which he first popularized the phrase "It is to laugh"; in "The Telephone Girl," "All on Account of Eliza," "The Red Kloof," "Hoch the Consul," at Weber and Fields's, and in "The Second Fiddle" and "The Man Who Stood Still." During this time he gave skilful portrayals of French character as Le Bardy in "The Girl of the Barracks" and Jean Poujol in "Julie Bon-Bon."

IN "RICHARD CARVEL."

IN "UNDER THE RED ROBE."

IN "THE WOLF."

IN "MAN AND SUPERMAN."

IN "THE SECOND IN COMMAND."

MISS IDA CONQUEST

IDA CONQUEST is an actress who after her first appearances on the stage advanced herself to a position among the popular leading women in America and she has maintained herself there by a long series of performances which have distinguished her as an artist of charm and ability. Born in Boston in 1870, she made her first appearance in New York at the Fifth Avenue Theatre January 28, 1893, as the First Girl Friend in "The Harvest." Olga Nethersole came to America in the next year and Miss Conquest played the ingénue parts in her repertoire at Palmer's Theatre.

The excellence of these performances attracted Charles Frohman's attention and he engaged her for the Empire Theatre. In that company she played Clarice in Henry Arthur Jones's "The Masqueraders"; moved to Hoyt's Theatre for the run of "The Foundling" in which she played Alice Maynall, and then she returned to the Empire to play conspicuous parts in Jones's "Michael and His Lost Angel," Clyde Fitch's "Bohemia," the dramatization of Stanley Weyman's "Under the Red Robe," "A Man and His Wife," Paul Potter's "The Conquerors," and Hudson Chambers's "The Tyranny of Tears." She created Dorothy Manners as John Drew's leading lady in the dramatization of Winston Churchill's "Richard Carvel."

Since then Miss Conquest has been conspicuous for many fine performances, notably as Mrs. Billings in Gillette's "Too Much Johnson," Gertrude West in the same writer's "Because She Loved Him So," as Muriel Mannering in Captain Marshall's "The Second in Command," as Helena in a production of "A Midsummer Night's Dream," which dedicated the New Amsterdam Theatre, as the Tzaritza in Richard Mansfield's production of Alexis Tolstoï's "Ivan the Terrible," as William Collier's leading woman during his first London season, as Ann Whitfield in Bernard Shaw's "Man and Superman," as the Comtesse de Roquelaure with Kyrle Bellew in Conan Doyle's "Brigadier Gerard," as a star in "The Moneymakers" and as Hilda McTavish in "The Wolf."

Miss Charlotte Walker

IN "ON PAROLE"
Photo by Hall

CHARLOTTE WALKER is a native of Texas and was born in the city of Galveston. Her first appearances in plays were as an amateur in her native city. With pronounced talent, as well as delicate beauty, and real charm, she adopted acting as a profession. She went to New York in 1895 and secured an interview with Richard Mansfield, who admitted her to his company. After a season of this valuable training she crossed to England and in the summer of 1896 acted with Charles Hawtry in "The Mummy." On her return she married and retired from the stage.

The call of the theatre was persistent, however, and she finally heeded it in 1900. Since that time she has been continuously prominent. Her re-appearance was made in "Miss Printt," with Marie Dressler, and for a short time she played with James A. Herne in "Sag Harbor." Then began a long association with James K. Hackett with whom she played in "Don Cæsar's Return," "The Crisis," "John Ermine of the Yellowstone," "The Crown Prince," "The Fortunes of the King," and "The House of Silence." This sequence was only once interrupted when she appeared with Kyrle Bellew in "A Gentleman of France."

Miss Walker has since created many leading parts in New York productions for which she is well remembered and much admired. The list includes Thora Neilson in "The Prodigal Son," Madge Bender in "The Embassy Ball," with Lawrence D'Orsay; Alice Travers in "The Prince Chap," and Agatha in "The Warrens of Virginia."

During two recent summers at the head of her own stock company, in Washington, D. C., Miss Walker broadened the range of her experience by hastily studied but effectively composed performances of Nora in "A Doll's House," Lady Windemere in "Lady Windemere's Fan," "Zaza," and other diversified characters. She is the wife of Eugene Walter, the dramatist, who has written "Just a Wife," for her.

Miss Charlotte Walker

IN "THE FORTUNE OF THE KING"

IN
"THE WARRENS OF
VIRGINIA"

SVENGALI

JEAN VALJEAN
IN "THE LAW AND THE MAN"

IN "CHILDREN OF THE GHETTO"

IN "THE BATTLE"

IN "DR. BELGRAFF"

Mr. WILTON LACKAYE

WILTON LACKAYE was born in Loudon County, Virginia, and was educated at the College of Ottawa and at Georgetown University. His first choice of a career was the priesthood, and in pursuit of this intention he and his father had reached New York on their way to Rome where he was to study at the Propaganda. Two weeks of theatre-going changed that plan. He felt the call of the stage. His family opposed him. They compromised on a legal career. There was in Washington an amateur organization known as the Lawrence Barrett Dramatic Society, and Lackaye became the president, though he was only eighteen years old at the time. Lawrence Barrett attended one of their performances and offered Lackaye a place in his company. He accepted and his father refused to speak to him.

This was in 1883 and for seven years he worked through a chaotic experience of all kinds of touring, stock work, and everything except idleness. During the year 1890 he acted Jack Adams in "Money Mad," Antonio in "A Mighty Power," Jim Hogan in "The Canuck," Pierre Clemenceau in "The Clemenceau Case," Dr. William Brown in "Dr. Bill," Claudius Nero in "Nero" and Captain Walsh in "The Haunted Room." After acting Pierre with Kate Claxton in "The Two Orphans" and creating Steve Carson in "The Power of the Press," he went to England and spent a year playing with George Alexander in "The Idler."

From the time he returned Mr. Lackaye took a firm position as one of the most able leading men and character actors on the American stage. His notable impersonations were Jefferson Stockton in Bronson Howard's "Aristocracy," John Stratton in Augustus Thomas's "New Blood"; Svengali in Paul Potter's dramatization of George DuMaurier's "Trilby"; Reb Shemuel in Israel Zangwill's "Children of the Ghetto"; Petronius in the dramatization of Sienkiewicz's "Quo Vadis?" and Richard Sterling in Clyde Fitch's "The Climbers."

He made an artistic but ineffectual effort at stardom in Charles Klein's "Dr. Belgraff" in 1897, but his fixed place was attained as Curtis Jadwin in Channing Pollock's dramatization of Frank Norris's "The Pit" in the winter of 1903. Since then Mr. Lackaye has acted Consul Bervick in Ibsen's "The Pillars of Society," Jean Valjean and M. Madeline in his own play "The Law and the Man," from Victor Hugo's "Les Misérables"; Hall Caine's "The Bondman," and finally as Haggleton in Cleveland Moffett's "The Battle."

MR. WILTON LACKAYE

IN "THE MARRIAGE OF WILLIAM ASHE"

IN "PRETTY PEGGY"

IN "A WOMAN'S WAY"
Photograph by Hall

IN "ABIGAIL"

MISS GRACE GEORGE

THE final acceptance of Grace George as one of our best actresses is an example of perseverance in the face of disheartening opinion that will encourage the steadfast and blight the weak of heart. She was a star for eight years before she came into a real position. The reason is near the surface. Miss George is that rarest of gifted creatures, a comedienne, and yet season after season she was advanced in rôles supposed to be light but in effect rather well saturated with emotion and in situations often automatic and theatrical. In 1907, however, she somehow made her appearance as Cyprienne in "Divorçons," and stood revealed. She played this rôle in London in the spring of that year and established herself there in a night. This effort was wisely followed by another comedy, Thomas Buchanan's "A Woman's Way," in which she played Marion Stanton, further obliterating earlier indiscretions of management, and in December, 1909, she acted Lady Teazle in "The School For Scandal" as guest player at The New Theatre and scored an emphatic success with both critics and public.

Miss George is a New York girl. After a few years in a convent school she prepared for a career on the stage at the American Academy of Dramatic Arts and gained her first professional experience in appearances on tour in Belasco and Fyle's military play, "The Girl I Left Behind Me." It was in a small part in an imported English farce, "The New Boy," presented June 23, 1894, at the Standard Theatre, that she made her New York debut. For three years she played a variety of parts on tour and in vaudeville. She returned to New York in 1898 and began to be heard of for her performances in "The Turtle" and "Mlle. Fi-Fi."

The following year she was advanced as a star in "The Countess Chiffon," an adaptation of the younger Dumas's "Diana de Lys." Her next plays were "Her Majesty," in 1900; "Under Southern Skies" during the two years following, together with a few performances in "Frou-Frou" and "Pretty Peggy" in 1903. Miss George acted Louise in the revival of "The Two Orphans" in 1904; Abigail Stokes in "Abigail" in the spring of 1905, and in the autumn following Lady Kitty in a dramatization of "The Marriage of William Ashe"; and "The Richest Girl" and Olivia Sherwood in "Clothes" in 1906. This was followed by her charming Cyprienne, in both America and England, Marion Stanton and Lady Teazle, which have made her future so well worth watching for the promise it holds of high pleasures for lovers of pure comedy.

MR. NAT C. GOODWIN

Copyright 1906 by Frank C. Bangs

N. C. GOODWIN, or "Nat" Goodwin, as he has been familiarly referred to for years, has enjoyed as great a popularity as any other actor in the American theatre. The talent for comedy which he brought to the stage was genuine and native, for he was a star from almost the beginning of his association with the playhouse. He was born in Boston in 1857. At school his gifts as a mimic were the admiration of the other pupils.

He made his professional appearance at the Boston Howard Athenæum as a newsboy in "Law in New York," March 5, 1874, after he had a brief career as a dry goods clerk and an upholsterer. His imitations rather than original characterization were his earliest stock in trade, and they were popular. He did much developing work in stock companies and burlesques such as "Black-Eyed Susan," and in 1876 he played LeBlanc in "Evangeline" and continued to act this rôle for two years.

He starred from this time on, and the list of farces, comedies, operas and dramas in which he appeared seems interminable, but it is interesting in recalling the large number of familiar titles his rich fun made popular: "Cruets," "Hobbies," "The Member from Slocum," Mathias Irving in "Those Bells," Ananias in "Warranted," Blizzard in "Confusion," "The Skating Rink," "A Terrible Time," "Little Jack Sheppard," "Turned Up," "The Mascot," "Lend Me Five Shillings," Gringoire in "A Royal Revenge," "A Gold Mine," "The Stowaway," "The Bookmaker," "The Nominee," "A Gilded Fool," Jim Radburn in Augustus Thomas's "In Mizzoura," "David Garrick," Bob Acres in "The Rivals," and Sir Lucius O'Trigger to Jefferson's Bob Acres, Cruger in "An American Citizen," Teddy North in Fitch's "The Cowboy and the Lady," Richard Carewe in "When We Were Twenty-One," Shylock in "The Merchant of Venice," Richard Arbuthnot in "The Altar of Friendship," Clyde Fitch's "Nathan Hale," Bottom in "A Midsummer Night's Dream," which was the dedicatory play of the New Amsterdam Theatre; Edwin Milton Royle's "My Wife's Husbands," "The Usurper," Captain James Barley in "Beauty and the Barge," Cherokee in "Wolfville," "The Genius," "In a Blaze of Glory," "The Easterner," "The Master Hand" and Mr. Tarkington and Mr. Harry Wilson's "Cameo Kirby."

He made his first appearance in London in July, 1890, in "The Gold Mine." He visited Australia in 1896, and made a second visit to London in 1899 and a third in 1906, acting several of his more admired comedies. At the noted Cincinnati Dramatic Festival Mr. Goodwin was the Modus in "The Hunchback" and the First Grave Digger in "Hamlet."

MR NAT C   GOODWIN

NATHAN HALE
Copyright 1899 Rockwood

BOB ACRES IN "THE RIVALS"

IN "IN MIZZOURA"

SHYLOCK
Copyright 1901 by Burr McIntosh

IN "THE BEAUTY AND THE BARGE"

IN "THE COWBOY AND THE LADY"

BOTTOM IN "A MIDSUMMER-NIGHT'S DREAM"

IN "THE BEAUTY AND THE BARGE"

"MISS BERTHA KALICH"

BERTHA KALICH acted the entire repertoire of Bernhardt and Duse during a long period in New York before that city can be said to have known of her existence. One night in May, 1905, at the conclusion of a season of stock performances at the American Theatre, on the invitation of George Fawcett, she played Sardou's "Fedora" with his company in English. The occasion was electric with the sense of discovery, for a great artist stood revealed. Yet behind that one performance was a long career of study, experience, and triumph.

During ten years Madame Kalich had been the leading actress at Bowery theatres for the quarter of a million Yiddish in that not unknown city referred to vaguely as "the East Side." Back of that decade was another spent in the Jewish theatres of Europe. After her eventful début in the new tongue she took a conspicuous place among the emotional and tragic actresses of the American stage. She made many ambitious appeals to the public at large, but, though appreciation was not withheld by the discriminating, the plays she acted in did not become popular, and after four years she temporarily retired.

Madame Kalich was born in the city of Lemberg of orthodox Jewish parents. The family was poor, and the daughter, after a brief term in school, joined the chorus of the Polish theatre, and soon was entrusted with parts. About the same time the Jewish Theatre was established, and before she was seventeen she was leading woman there and had acted a long series of tragic rôles. Then for three years she played in Roumania and Hungary. The manager of a Yiddish theatre in New York found her in Roumania and persuaded her to become the star of his company. She accepted because she felt it might lead to the other stage, which finally did welcome her.

After leaving the Ghetto, Madame Kalich acted "Monna Vanna" in Sudermann's play of that name at the Manhattan Theatre in 1905. She followed this with a dramatization of Tolstoi's "Kreutzer Sonata," Angel Guimera's "Marta of the Lowlands," a production of Percy Mackaye's "Sappho and Phaon," and Thomas Dickinson's "The Unbroken Road."

LA TOSCA

IN "MARTA OF THE LOWLANDS"

IN "MONNA VANNA"

MISS BERTHA KALICH

AS SAPPHO IN "SAPPHO AND PHAON"

MR. DOUGLAS FAIRBANKS

DOUGLAS FAIRBANKS is generally regarded as the leading exponent of light comedy boys and young men of to-day. He has an ingratiating personality charged with health, directness, breeziness, and a certain patrician quality which contributes an attraction to any part he plays. He has been on the stage only nine years, yet in that time he has created a new rôle in New York on an average of at least once a year.

Mr. Fairbanks was born in Colorado and went on the stage in 1899, in support of Frederick Warde, playing small parts in that actor's Shakespearian repertoire. He soon doffed the romantic costume, however, and has since been seen only in modern dress. He made his début at the Manhattan Theatre in 1900, in support of Herbert Kelcey and Effie Shannon as the young lover, Lord Canning, in Martha Morton's "Her Lord and Master." The play passed and Fairbanks remained. The next season he acted small parts in "The Rose of Plymouth Town" and "Mrs. Jack."

Landry Court was the first character in which he had a real chance to score and he attained a fixed position by his performance of it. This was in Channing Pollock's dramatization of Frank Norris's "The Pit," in Wilton Lackaye's company in the spring of 1904. He played in "Two Little Sailor Boys," and when "Fantana" ran at the Lyric, he took his first and last dip into musical comedy.

The next time he appeared he was "featured" in "A Case of Frenzied Finance." It was not for long. A part in "As Ye Sow" reacquainted him with touring in 1905. During the summer of 1906 he acted a round of juvenile parts in one of the summer stock companies for which Denver has for many years been famous, and when he returned to New York in the fall he created Thomas Smith, Jr., with Grace George in "Clothes." Two of his most conspicuous hits sandwiched a failure in his successive appearances as Perry Carter Wainwright in "The Man of the Hour," as a star in "All for a Girl" and playing the secretary as a co-star with Thomas A. Wise in "A Gentleman From Mississippi."

IN "THE MAN OF THE HOUR"

IN "ALL FOR A GIRL"

IN "A GENTLEMAN FROM MISSISSIPPI"

IN "A CASE OF FRENZIED FINANCE"

IN "PIERRE OF THE PLAINS."   IN "THE TRAVELLING SALESMAN."

IN "THE BATTLE."   IN "SUCH A LITTLE QUEEN."

Miss ELSIE FERGUSON

ELSIE FERGUSON became a celebrity from the night of her first appearance as "Such a Little Queen," for everyone who has seen her thinks that title fits the actress as well as the character. Of course there was an Elsie Ferguson before that, and many people saw her, but few remembered her by name, for the mass of theatregoers are oblivious of names unless they are burned into their consciousness in electric light or stamped in very large black type.

Miss Ferguson's rise suggests how surprisingly few daughters of New York families achieve distinction on the stage. She was born in the big city where actresses are made. Her father was of Scotch, her mother of German descent. It was planned that she should become a teacher and she attended a normal school for a while, but fate was working in another direction. Because her shoulders were rounding, her mother had her join a fencing class. There she met a girl who knew an actress, and the sequel is obvious.

Miss Ferguson made her first appearance on the stage in 1900 in the chorus of "The Belle of New York," on tour. She remained in the chorus of musical comedy companies for four years, and then left both chorus and music behind her for a part in support of Louis Mann in "The Second Fiddle." But it was not yet for good and all, for during the season of 1905 she sang Celeste in "Miss Dolly Dollars," in Lulu Glaser's company.

Since then she has been acting parts of steadily increasing importance. Following a short term as Caroline in "Julie Bon-Bon," again with Louis Mann, she played Agnes in "Brigadier Gerard" with Kyrle Bellew; Ella Seaford in "The Earl of Pawtucket" with Cyril Maude, at the Playhouse, London; Greeba in "The Bondman" with Wilton Lackaye; Jean Galbraith in "Pierre of the Plains" with Edgar Selwyn; Jenny Moran with Mr. Lackaye in "The Battle," and Beth Elliott in James Forbes's comedy, "The Travelling Salesman." In the autumn of 1909 she won wide admiration as a star as Queen Anna Victoria in Channing Pollock's comedy, "Such a Little Queen."

GLORY QUAYLE
IN "THE CHRISTIAN"

ROSALIND

Miss Viola Allen

SISTER GIOVANNA

VIOLA ALLEN attained to a conspicuous position earlier in life than any other living American actress who has augmented her fame as the years have passed. Her career covers two generations for, though in youth and achievements she belongs to the present generation, she was leading lady for John McCullough, Lawrence Barrett and Tommaso Salvini, who belonged to quite another period. The explanation is simple. Miss Allen played their Cordelia, Virginia, Parthenia, Desdemona, Julia, and Lady Anne when she was but fifteen years old.

She was born October 27, 1869, in Huntsville, Alabama, and was educated in Boston, Toronto, and New York. It was not her intention to go on the stage. One day, while "Esmeralda" was enjoying its great vogue at the Madison Square Theatre, Annie Russell, who was playing the title part, fell ill. Her father was a member of the company, and William Seymour, the stage manager of the theatre, asked him to allow his daughter, Viola, to play the part. It was in this play, part, and theatre that she made her début, July 4, 1882. This performance attracted the attention of John McCullough, who made her his leading lady in 1884. Then followed the engagements as leading woman for Salvini and Barrett. Miss Allen has always shown marked versatility in her range of parts, and after this experience in poetic rôles, she turned with facility to the modern rôles of the Boston Museum. She was chosen next to play Lydia Languish and Cecily Homespun in "The Rivals" and "The Heir at Law" when Joseph Jefferson and William J. Florence made their joint starring tour. After an interval in New York productions of modern plays, she joined the Empire Theatre Company in 1893 and remained five years. She created the leading woman's part in the American productions of "Liberty Hall," "The Younger Son," "The Councilor's Wife," "Sowing the Wind," "Gudgeons," "The Masqueraders," "John-a-Dreams," "The Importance of Being Earnest," "Michael and His Lost Angel," "A Woman's Reason," "Marriage," "Bohemia," "The Highwayman," "Under the Red Robe," "A Man and His Wife," and "The Conquerors."

In 1898 she made her stellar début as Glory Quayle in Hall Caine's "The Christian." Since then she has acted Dolores in Marion Crawford's "In the Palace of the King," Julia in Sheridan Knowles's "The Hunchback," Roma in Hall Caine's "The Eternal City," Viola in "Twelfth Night," Imogen in "Cymbeline," Hermione and Perdita in "The Winter's Tale," Mistress Betty in Clyde Fitch's "The Toast of the Town," in "Irene Wycherley," Rosalind in "As You Like It" and in Marion Crawford's "The White Sister." Miss Allen has never played any other than the leading woman's or the star part.

Miss Viola Allen

IN "THE WINTER'S TALE"   JULIET   IN "THE WINTER'S TALE"

IN "THE MUSKETEERS"

MR. JAMES O'NEIL

IN "THE MANXMAN"

ALTHOUGH James O'Neil is one of the most admired and forceful actors of mature parts on the American stage to-day and he is best known to this generation for his many performances of "Monte Cristo," his beginnings were at the elbow of the giants of the classic period of our theatre's history, and the variety and prominence of his own accomplishments in his prime furnish one of the inspiring records in that same history.

Mr. O'Neil was born in Kilkenny, Ireland, in 1849. He was brought across the Atlantic when young and during the Civil War he sold uniforms in his brother-in-law's store in Norfolk, Virginia. His desire to become an actor was fired by the wartime performances he saw at the old theatre in the Virginia seaport. In those days the great stars traveled alone and played with stock companies in the principal cities. Mr. O'Neil first acted with one of these companies at the National Theatre in Cincinnati, then with Ford's in Baltimore, and with McVicker's in Chicago as leading man at twenty-three. During these engagements he supported Charlotte Cushman, Edwin Forrest, Edwin Booth and Adelaide Neilson who said he was the best Romeo she had ever had. His next move was to Hooley's Theatre, in the same city, as a stock star and thence direct to San Francisco where, at the Baldwin, he was for three years the most admired actor in the city.

Here, much against his will, he participated in one of the turbulent sensations of stage history. The Passion Play was produced and he was persuaded to play the part of Christ. For this the whole country was aroused and he was imprisoned. He was released shortly and fined fifty dollars "for a misdemeanor" and Henry E. Abbey engaged him to come to New York and act the same rôle. But public protests prevented and instead Mr. O'Neil entered upon a three years' stay at A. M. Palmer's Union Square Theatre in leading parts. The fame of this theatre was then at its height. Mr. O'Neil made his début there in a revival of "The Two Orphans," October 2, 1876. Among the rôles he created were Maurice in "Miss Moulton," with Clara Morris, and Vladimir in "The Danicheffs." As early as April 21, 1875, when a stock star at Hooley's Theatre in Chicago, he acted the leading rôle in Fechter's version of Dumas's "The Count of Monte Cristo" and in 1883 he acted it again in San Francisco with only three rehearsals. The critics damned it, but he later rehearsed it carefully and produced it in such a way as to make it the extraordinary success it has been. No American actor has played one rôle oftener than James O'Neil has played Edmond Dantès unless Joseph Jefferson rivaled his record with Rip Van Winkle.

Mr. O'Neil's later efforts have all been in the way of releasing himself from the demand for this character and he has given many fine and interesting performances, notably D'Artagnan in "The Musketeers," in "The Manxman," "Brigadier Gerard," and "Virginius." His latest performance is in support of Viola Allen in Marion Crawford's "The White Sister," as Monsignore Saracinnesca, which reveals a beautiful and ripened art.

Miss OLIVE WYNDHAM

IN "THE MAN FROM HOME"

IN "A COTTAGE IN THE AIR"

Photograph by Frank C. Bangs

OLIVE WYNDHAM is one of the youngest players in a leading position on the stage to-day, and her career is correspondingly brief. But what she lacks in experience she supplies in a girlish but patrician beauty, winsome personality, and a definite talent for such rôles as she has played.

Miss Wyndham was born in Chicago and was educated there. When a mere child she showed a special gift for imitations and at one time she repeated Vesta Tilley's whole repertoire of songs in a manner that left little to choose between the gifted original and the clever imitator. She met Margaret Anglin and other celebrated players in her own home and, when she and her sister had finished their studies, they both decided to adopt a career on the stage. Janet Beecher is the name assumed by her sister.

Miss Wyndham's first professional appearance was with Kyrle Bellew in a small part in "Raffles." From this she stepped at once into a leading part as Ethel Granger-Simpson in Booth Tarkington and Harry L. Wilson's "The Man From Home," which she created at the Studebaker Theatre, Chicago, in 1908. She played this part until the termination of the long New York run and then went to The New Theatre. In that company her first parts were the Princess Priscilla in the production of "The Cottage in the Air," and Maria in the revival of Sheridan's "School for Scandal."

Mr LEW FIELDS

THE name of Lew Fields immediately suggests the name of Joe Weber, for they were partners for twenty-seven years and the public knew no separate identity of the famous comedy team of Weber and Fields. They were both born on the East Side in New York city and attended the public schools there. In 1877, while still in their teens, they formed a partnership and appeared together on the variety stages of the East Side. Fields was "the tall one" and Weber "the little one" and as the "Dutch Senators" they were celebrated for their dialect comedy. Eight years later they formed a company of their own and for eleven years toured the country at its head.

In 1896 they leased a small music hall on Twenty-ninth Street, built a Broadway entrance, renamed it Weber and Fields's Broadway Music Hall and began to give a series of burlesques on current theatrical attractions, which prospered instantly and continuously for eight years. The company was made up of the most gifted burlesque and comic opera favorites of the period. In the initial cast were Sam Bernard, Ross and Fenton, John T. Kelly, Yolande Wallace, and Frankie Bailey. David Warfield, DeWolf Hopper, Willie Collier, "Pete" Dailey, Louis Mann, Fay Templeton, Lillian Russell, Lulu Glaser, William Hodge, and May Irwin were all members of the company, some of them for many seasons in succession. The sequence of their principal burlesques was "Pousse Café," "Hurly Burly," "Whirl-I-Gig," "Fiddle-Dee-Dee," "Hoity-Toity," "Twirly Whirly," and "Whoop-de-Doo." The pieces were chiefly written by Edgar Smith, the music by John Stromberg, and they were staged by Julian Mitchell.

The partnership was dissolved in 1904. Mr. Weber continued to play in the same house, renamed Weber's Theatre. Mr. Fields opened Fields's Theatre, now the Hackett, and appeared as a star in "It Happened in Nordland." He has since leased the Herald Square Theatre and his engagements have been played there in "About Town," "The Girl Behind the Counter" and "Old Dutch."

IN "THE BEAUTY SPOT"

Miss MARGUERITE CLARK

MARGUERITE CLARK is one of the promising young actresses for whom her admirers entertain high hopes on the plane of dainty, light, popular comedy. There is not a great deal of this young lady in inches, but she enjoys an uncommonly large share of beauty, girlish charm, grace and personality. Her first venture as a star did not give her the opportunity necessary to achieve a permanent position, but there will no doubt be other opportunities.

Miss Clark is a Cincinnati girl. Her first experience on the stage was in the chorus of the Strakosch Opera Company while that organization was playing a repertoire of standard light opera in Baltimore. Other engagements in stock opera companies followed until she won the chance to understudy Irene Bentley in "The Belle of Bohemia." After that one performance rôles of slowly increasing importance were given her in "The Burgomaster," in Dan Daly's support in "The New Yorkers" and in "The Wild Rose."

Her first real prominence, however, was gained in De Wolf Hopper's support as Polly in "Mr. Pickwick," which she sang, danced and acted more daintily and gracefully than the stage had known in a long time before. After brief experiences as Contrary Mary in "Babes in Toyland" and as Mataya, the white-flanneled Crown Prince in a revival of "Wang," she created Sylvia in "Happyland," accenting previous pleasant impressions. When Mr. Hopper produced "The Pied Piper" she was Elvira, and in "The Beauty Spot" during the winter of 1908 she played Nadine. In the fall of 1909 she was put forward as a star in "The Wishing Ring," a comedy without music, for which she prepared herself in a measure during the preceding summer in leading girl parts in a dramatic stock company in St. Louis.

Miss JULIA MARLOWE

JULIA MARLOWE has played a varied list of characters, but her fame rests on her beautiful impersonations of the heroines of romance and the women of Shakespeare. While she has acted Parthenia, Juliet, and Ophelia she has been without a peer in these rôles.

Miss Marlowe was born Sarah Frances Frost, at Caldbeck, England. She came to America with her parents when a young girl, in 1875, and studied in Cincinnati and Kansas City schools. Her first professional appearance was made at Ironton, Ohio, in 1882, as a sailor in "H. M. S. Pinafore" in one of the juvenile opera companies which were at that time the vogue. She was soon promoted to the rôle of Sir Joseph Porter and leading rôles in other operas. After a brief experience in support of Robert McWade she came under the instruction of Ada Dow and made her first appearance as a star as Parthenia, at Bayonne, N. J., in 1887. Her talent, charm and beauty were at once recognized and she quickly grew into the affection of the whole country.

The list of Miss Marlowe's characters is notable and includes Pauline in "The Lady of Lyons," Constance in "The Love Chase," Viola in "Twelfth Night," Rosalind in "As You Like It," Julia in "The Hunchback," Galatea, Imogen in "Cymbeline," Charles Hart in "Rogues and Vagabonds," Juliet, Kate Hardcastle in "She Stoops To Conquer," Prince Hal in "King Henry IV." (part i.), Mary in "For Bonnie Prince Charlie," Lydia Languish in "The Rivals," "Chatterton," "Countess Valeska," "Colinette," "Barbara Frietchie," Mary Tudor in "When Knighthood Was In Flower," Charlotte in "The Cavalier," "Queen Fiametta," Lady Bancaster in "Fools of Nature," Beatrice in "Much Ado About Nothing," Ophelia in "Hamlet," Katherine in "The Taming of the Shrew," Portia in "The Merchant of Venice," "Jeanne d'Arc," Rautendelein in "The Sunken Bell," Salome in "John the Baptist," "Gloria," Yvette in "The Goddess of Reason," and Cleopatra in "Antony and Cleopatra."

Miss Marlowe was married in May, 1894, to the late Robert Taber, at the time her leading man, and for a brief period she was known professionally as Julia Marlowe Taber. In the autumn of 1904 she became a co-star with E. H. Sothern and since that time they have acted together almost continuously. When the New Theatre was dedicated in November, 1909, Miss Marlowe was a guest player and acted Cleopatra in the initial production.

Miss JULIA MARLOWE

ROSALIND

IN "TWELFTH NIGHT"
Copyright 1892 by B. J. Falk

OPHELIA

IN "THE GODDESS OF REASON"

IN "THE LITTLE CORPORAL."

IN "WHEN KNIGHTS WERE BOLD."

MR. FRANCIS WILSON

IN "WHEN KNIGHTS WERE BOLD."

FRANCIS WILSON, after a long career on the stage identified intimately with low comedy tactics in comic opera, demonstrated that it is possible for an actor with the native gifts, determination and zeal, to raise himself to popularity on the plane of more legitimate comedy without music or song or the alluring support of a chorus of beauties. He demonstrated this by doing it.

For five years Mr. Wilson has been a successful star in straight light comedy. Before then he was a leading and then a star comedian in comic opera for twenty-two years. His first efforts were in small character comedy parts in the stock company at the Chestnut Street Theatre, Philadelphia, where he made his first appearance on the stage, in 1878, in a performance of "London Assurance." He was born in the same city in February 1854. He made his debut in New York in 1889 in "Our Goblins." His next parts were Sam Gerridge in "Caste," Sergeant in "Ours" and Sir Joseph Porter in "H. M. S. Pinafore." His success as the First Lord of the Admiralty sealed his future for over twenty years. Comic opera claimed him, and he was unsurpassed in his popularity during this time.

The list of the productions in which Mr. Wilson's fun was exploited recalls some of the merriest moments in the theatre. At first he was a member of the companies, for the greater part of the time at the Casino, which produced "The Queen's Lace Handkerchief," "The Princess of Trebizonde," "Prince Methusalem," "Nanon," "Amorita," "The Gypsy Baron," "Erminie," in which his Cadeaux or "Caddy" became a comic opera classic; and then headed his own company in "The Oolah," "The Merry Monarch," "The Lion Tamer," "The Devil's Deputy," "The Chieftain," "Half a King," "The Little Corporal," "Cyrano de Bergerac," "The Monks of Malabar," "The Strollers," and "The Toreador." During this time, in the spring of 1896, he acted David in Joseph Jefferson's all-star revival of "The Rivals."

Mr. Wilson abandoned comic opera in 1903, when he acted "Cousin Billy," though he continued to star. His rôles since have been Père Marlotte in "The Little Father of the Wilderness," Montague Silsey in "The Mountain Climber," Sir Guy de Vere in "When Knights Were Bold," and Tom Beach in his own comedy "The Bachelor's Baby." Mr. Wilson is the author of "The Eugene Field I Knew," "Recollections of a Fellow Player" (Joseph Jefferson), and several comedies.

MR. FRANCIS WILSON

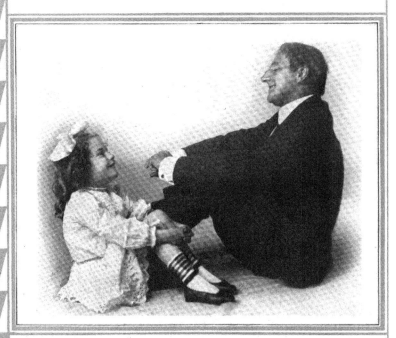

IN "THE LITTLE CORPORAL." IN "THE OOLAH." IN "THE LITTLE CORPORAL."

Miss BLANCHE WALSH

IN "MARCELLE"

LA TOSCA

IN "THE TEST"

MISS BLANCHE WALSH'S association with the professional stage dates from her sixteenth year and she has acted rôles of steadily increasing importance and matured her technique with skillful improvement until she has fixed herself as a stellar actress of power and worth.

Miss Walsh was born in New York City in 1873 and made her professional début there in 1889 in a small part in "Siberia." She was immediately engaged for leading parts by Marie Wainwright, who at the time was playing a somewhat extensive repertoire, and in her first year on the stage played Queen Elizabeth in "Amy Robsart," Olivia in "Twelfth Night," Grace Harkaway in "London Assurance," and Madeline in "Frederic Lemaitre."

Her first really notable hit was as Diana Stockton, of which she was the original, in Bronson Howard's "Aristocracy." She soon became Nat Goodwin's leading lady and in 1895 created Mrs. Bulford in "The Great Diamond Robbery"; succeeded Virginia Harned as "Trilby" during the run of that play at the Garden Theatre, accompanied Nat Goodwin to Australia in 1896, played Edith Varney with William Gillette in "Secret Service," in London; acted Helen Le Grand when Sol Smith Russell produced "A Bachelor's Romance," at the Garden Theatre in 1897, and created Jeanne in "The Conquerors," at the Empire in 1898.

Miss Walsh began to star on tour that same year and for some time made a specialty of the Sardou repertoire, acting in "La Tosca," "Fedora," "Cleopatra," and "Gismonda." Long tours and varied experiments with new plays followed until 1903, when she created Katusha in "Resurrection" and her subtle, finished, highly characterized performance of this part brought her to a position she has since maintained with other fine creations. Her plays here have been "The Kreutzer Sonata," "A Woman in the Case," Clyde Fitch's "The Straight Road," and Jules E. Goodman's "The Test."

ROMEO

IN "THE TEST" Miss BLANCHE WALSH

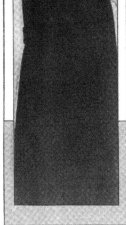

IN "RESURRECTION"

IN "LA TOSCA" CLEOPATRA

IN "GISMONDA"
Copyright 1899 by J. Schloss

MERCUTIO IN "ROMEO AND JULIET"

MR JAMES K HACKETT

IN "THE PRIDE OF JENNICO"
Copyright 1900 by Burr McIntosh

CHARLES STUART IN "THE FORTUNES OF THE KING"

IN "DON CÆSAR'S RETURN"   STEPHEN BRICE IN "THE CRISIS"   JOHN ERMINE

JAMES K. HACKETT, the son of James H. Hackett, the celebrated Falstaff of his time, was born on Wolfe Island, Ontario, September 6, 1869. While a student of the College of the City of New York, he was the leading spirit in student theatricals. He was graduated in 1891, and studied law, but after a year he decided on the theatre as a career.

His first professional appearance was made in Philadelphia, in March, 1892, as François in "The Broken Seal," and, after a variety of experiences, including a season as leading man for Lotta, and another in Augustin Daly's company, he made two successes as de Neipperg in "Madame Sans-Gêne" at the Broadway Theatre, and as Count de Charney in "The Queen's Necklace" with Mrs. Potter at Daly's in November the same year.

This opened the way for his later career of activities as leading man, star and manager. He went to the Lyceum in 1895, and, on Mr. Kelcey's resignation in 1896, he became leading man of the company. He acted the leading rôles in "The Home Secretary," a revival of "The Prisoner of Zenda," "The Marriage of Leonie," "The Late Mr. Costello," "The Wife of Willoughby," "The First Gentleman of Europe," "The Mayflower," "The Princess and the Butterfly," "The Tree of Knowledge," and "Rupert of Hentzau." Mr. Hackett also acted Romeo to Olga Nethersole's Juliet, and Mercutio to Maude Adams's Juliet.

In March, 1900, he made his début as a star at the Criterion Theatre as Jennico in "The Pride of Jennico," and has since appeared at the head of his own company as Don Cæsar de Bazan in "Don Cæsar's Return," in "A Chance Ambassador," as Stephen Brice in "The Crisis," as John Ermine in "John Ermine of the Yellowstone," Prince Robert in "The Crown Prince," Charles Stuart in "The Fortunes of the King," Victor in "The House of Silence," Jack Frobisher in "The Walls of Jericho," as John Glayde in "John Glayde's Honor," and as Maurice Brachard in "Samson."

In addition to acting and managing his own company, he has produced several plays, and is the lessee of the Hackett Theatre, in New York City.

Miss JULIA SANDERSON

JULIA SANDERSON is one of the attractive leading young women of musical comedy whose name in the cast means a beautiful, graceful and attractive girl on the stage. She has been before the public only a few years, which seem fewer since London has known her, for her time has been divided between America and England.

Miss Sanderson is the daughter of an actor, Albert Sackett, and was born in Springfield, Mass. She made her first appearance on the stage in child parts with the Forepaugh Stock Company of Philadelphia and remained in that organization for five years.

That was her last association with drama. She next joined the chorus of "Winsome Winnie" where her pretty face and graceful ways attracted immediate attention and she was cast for a speaking part in "The Chinese Honeymoon." For a season she played Mataya, the Crown Prince of Siam, in De Wolf Hopper's revival of "Wang," then became immensely popular during the runs of "Fantana" and "The Tourists," and for a while sought the diversity of vaudeville.

When she returned to musical comedy in 1907 it was under Charles Frohman's management. He almost immediately presented her to London audiences, with whom she repeated her American success. Since then she has played at the head of Mr. Frohman's musical companies on both sides of the Atlantic. Her conspicuous successes have been made in "The Dairymaids," "The Honorable Phil," "Kitty Grey," and "The Arcadians."

MISS ADA REHAN

PORTIA
Copyright 1899 by A. Dupont

ROSALIND

PORTIA
Copyright 1899 by A. Dupont

ADA REHAN is of the line of Gwynne, Woffington, Oldfield, Nisbet and Terry. Attached to her long reign at Daly's are some of the rarest memories of the American stage. No one of that time equalled her as Katherine, the Shrew, or Rosalind, and she was not surpassed as the heroines of old comedy or the gay spirits of modern farce. She has acted little of recent years, but the theatre is richer for the hope that she may at any time return to disclose again that rarest of arts—true high comedy.

Miss Rehan was born in Limerick, Ireland, and was brought to America when five years old with her brother, Arthur, and her two sisters, Kate and Harriett, who afterwards became known as Mrs. Oliver Doud Byron and Hattie Russell. She followed her two sisters on the stage, making her first appearance in the company of her brother-in-law, Mr. Byron, as Clara in "Across the Continent," at Newark, N. J., in 1874. Her early engagements were in the stock companies in John Drew's Arch Street Theatre in Philadelphia, and in Louisville, Albany and Baltimore.

When, in 1879, Augustin Daly opened the theatre which still bears his name, Miss Rehan became the leading woman of his company and held her position until his death twenty years later. On this stage she played over 200 rôles. These included Katherine in Shakespeare's "The Taming of the Shrew," Rosalind in "As You Like It," Mistress Ford in "The Merry Wives of Windsor," Viola in "Twelfth Night," Portia in "The Merchant of Venice," Beatrice in "Much Ado About Nothing," Helena in "A Midsummer-Night's Dream," Julia in "The Two Gentlemen of Verona" and Miranda in "The Tempest." She created leading rôles in Mr. Daly's long series of farces from the French and German, and was a fascinating embodiment of Lady Teazle in "The School for Scandal," Peggy Thrift in "A Country Girl," Sylvia in "The Recruiting Officer," Lady Gay Spanker in "London Assurance," Julia in "The Hunchback," Letitia Hardy in "The Belle's Stratagem," Donna Volante in "The Wonder" and of other heroines of old comedies.

Since Mr. Daly's death she has emerged from her retirement twice, on one occasion to play Nell Gwynne in Paul Kester's comedy, "Sweet Nell of Old Drury," and on another occasion to star with Otis Skinner in Shakespearian comedies. Under Mr. Daly's management Miss Rehan acted in Paris, Berlin, Hamburg, London, Edinburgh, Dublin, Stratford-on-Avon and throughout Great Britain, with a distinction and acclaim unapproached by any other American actress before or since.

Mr FRANK KEENAN

FRANK KEENAN was born in Maine, he grew up in Iowa, was a clerk in Boston, owned a cigar store, tried amateur acting and finally made his first appearance on the professional stage at Richmond, in his native State, playing Archibald Carlyle in "East Lynne" for the munificent salary of nine dollars a week.

Hard, happy years of development followed in New England touring repertoire companies, in which the plays ranged from "Virginius" to a farce, and then he came under the direction of James A. Herne, who gave his talents their proper direction. For a year he played one of the leading parts in "McKenna's Flirtation." Securing a place in the company at the Boston Museum, he acted several prominent character parts there, then created Brother Paul in Viola Allen's production of "The Christian," and during the later days of stock performances at the Pike Opera House, Cincinnati, he was stage director.

He left this theatre to star on long tours in Sol Smith Russell's characters in "The Poor Relation," "Peaceful Alley" and "The Honorable John Grigsby." The last he acted at the Manhattan Theatre, in January, 1902. Vaudeville took him for a time and he left it to support Nance O'Neil during her first Boston engagement, playing Macbeth and other leading rôles.

Then followed an ambitious experiment, in the little house of experiments, the Berkeley Lyceum, in Forty-fourth Street, New York City. Mr. Keenan leased it and acted a number of serious one-act plays. The enterprise lasted only a month, but it revealed him an artist of such range and skill that he took his place at once among the important actors on our stage. On this thumb-nail stage he produced "The Threshold," "Strolling Players," which was a version of "I Pagliacci"; "The System of Dr. Tarr," "The Lady Bookie," "The Lady Across the Hall," and "The Passion in the Suburbs."

Mr. Keenan joined Blanche Bates for the production of "The Girl of the Golden West," in which he created the sheriff, Jack Rance. He was equally successful as General Warren in "The Warrens of Virginia," from which he passed to a stellar position in "On the Heights."

Miss MAUDE ADAMS

PETER PAN

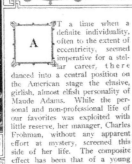

SUZANNE BLONDET IN "THE MASKED BALL"

A T a time when a definite individuality, often to the extent of eccentricity, seemed imperative for a stellar career, there danced into a central position on the American stage the elusive, girlish, almost elfish personality of Maude Adams. While the personal and non-professional life of our favorites was exploited with little reserve, her manager, Charles Frohman, without any apparent effort at mystery, screened this side of her life. The composite effect has been that of a young woman, dignified almost to the point of distinction by a sane, personal reserve, and endearing herself to her public by a constantly expanding gallery of charming and often notable characterizations.

Early in her career Miss Adams won her right to consideration by a valuable apprenticeship along varied lines. She made her début in her native Salt Lake City, when nine months old as a baby in arms, in "The Lost Child." As a child she also played Little Schneider in "Fritz" with J. K. Emmet. Her mother was an actress and she was acquainted with the stage from babyhood. She began to play young ladies about 1888, which is also the year of her first appearance in New York, in "The Paymaster." In quick succession she shifted from manager to manager, acting in "The Highest Bidder," "A Midnight Bell," and "All the Comforts of Home." In the last named engagement, in the fall of 1890, she found herself with Charles Frohman, and she has not since had any other manager. After inconspicuous rôles in "Men and Women" and "The Lost Paradise," she became John Drew's leading woman, appearing first with him in Palmer's Theatre, October 3, 1892, as Suzanne in "The Masked Ball," and afterwards in "Butterflies," "The Bauble Shop," "That Imprudent Young Couple," "Christopher, Jun.," "Rosemary" and "Too Happy by Half."

It was her winsome and irresistible performance of Dorothy in "Rosemary" which won her stellar consideration, and great indeed was the favor extended her as Lady Babbie in J. M. Barrie's "The Little Minister," played first in Washington in the autumn of 1897. The subsequent record is one of a large percentage of successes and a steady growth in popular affection until Maude Adams is probably the most loved of the public favorites. The definitive list includes Juliet; Rostand's "L'Aiglon;" "Quality Street," her second Barrie play; "The Pretty Sister of Jose"; "'Op o' Me Thumb"; "Peter Pan," her third Barrie play; "The Jesters"; and "What Every Woman Knows," the faithful Barrie's fourth play for Miss Adams.

NELL IN "THE LOST PARADISE"

IN "THE LITTLE MINISTER"

JULIET

IN "JOAN OF ARC"

IN "WHAT EVERY WOMAN KNOWS"

IN "L'AIGLON"

Copyright 1909 by Charles Frohman

MISS EFFIE SHANNON

AS a member of the old Lyceum Theatre stock company during its best days, Effie Shannon was the most admired ingénue on the stage. Later, in the same theatre, she made her début as a star and her charm and ability have since won sympathetic admiration. She and Herbert Kelcey, as co-stars, are among the most popular players in the country.

Miss Shannon made her first appearance on the stage as a child in a crowd of supers in John McCullough's revival of "Coriolanus" at the Boston Theatre, in the city of her birth. Her first speaking part was little Eva in "Uncle Tom's Cabin." For several years she was known as La Petite Shannon. She did not escape the juvenile "H. M. S. Pinafore" experience, and while still a child sang in the chorus of one of these companies for a time.

After a variety of inconsequential parts in various productions, she played and made conspicuous successes of Rose Leyburn in "Robert Elsmere," Titania in Daly's production of "A Midsummer Night's Dream," Jenny Buckthorn in the first production of "Shenandoah," before she joined the Lyceum company in 1889. During four years at this theatre she played the leading ingénue parts in "The Charity Ball," "The Idler," "Nerves," "The Open Gate," "The Old, Old Story," "Old Heads and Young Hearts," "Lady Bountiful," "Squire Kate," "White Roses," "Merry Gotham," "The Grey Mare," "Americans Abroad," and "The Guardsman."

For several years Miss Shannon supported Rose Coghlan, Mrs. Langtry, Olga Nethersole and W. H. Crane. Herbert Kelcey was leading man at the Lyceum during Miss Shannon's association with the company and in 1898 they joined forces again, this time as joint stars, and have remained together at the head of their own company since, to the genuine delight of an extensive public. They have acted in "The Moth and the Flame," "My Lady Dainty," "Manon Lescaut," "Her Lord and Master," "Taps," "Sherlock Holmes," "The Daughters of Men," "The Lightning Conductor," and "The Thief."

IN "HEDDA GABLER"

IN "THE DEVIL"
Photograph by Fronk C. Bangs

IN "THE ROSE"

MR GEORGE ARLISS

AMONG the actors whom England has of recent years sent to adorn the American stage George Arliss has won a high place. Recognition came to him immediately upon his appearance on this side of the Atlantic, for he brought his art ripened and polished by an extended experience.

Mr. Arliss first disclosed himself to his American admirers in 1901 as Cayley Drummle in "The Second Mrs. Tanqueray" and as the Duke of St. Olpherts in "The Notorious Mrs. Ebbsmith," in support of Mrs. Patrick Campbell on her first visit. David Belasco engaged him to remain and the next year he intensified the impression of his performances of the Pinero characters by his creation of the Japanese Prime Minister, Zakkuri, in John Luther Long and David Belasco's "The Darling of the Gods."

He passed, in 1904, to Mrs. Fiske's fine company and with her he remained until 1908, playing the Marquis of Steyne in "Becky Sharp," Raoul Berton in McClellan's "Leah Kleschna," Count Chotean de Rohan in Mrs. Fiske's one-act play, "The Rose"; M. d'Ancelor in another of her short plays, "The Eyes of the Heart"; Ulric Brendel in Ibsen's "Rosmersholm," and Sir William Cites-Derby in Langdon Mitchell's "The New York Idea."

A stellar position was reached by Mr. Arliss in the autumn of 1908 when he appeared at the Belasco Theatre in one of the several versions of "The Devil" which were epidemic at the moment. His performance carried the play past the transient interest at first excited by a spectacular controversy and after a long run in New York he played it on tour. In 1909 he created the title rôle in "Septimus," a dramatization by W. J. Locke of his own novel "Septimus."

Mr. Arliss was born in London, April 10, 1868, and his father was William Arliss-Andrews, a printer and publisher whose establishment was within a block of the British Museum. His first appearance on the stage was made in London at the Elephant and Castle in 1887. For many years he played all sorts of parts in the provinces, arriving on a first-class London stage only a short time before he came with Mrs. Campbell to America.

MR GEORGE ARLISS

IN "THE DARLING OF THE GODS"

IN "BECKY SHARP"

SEPTIMUS

BONITA IN "ARIZONA"

IN "MERELY MARY ANN"

Miss ELEANOR ROBSON

THIS country has so heartily and completely adopted Eleanor Robson and this charming actress has so entirely adopted America that, if known, the fact is quite forgotten that she is an English girl. Miss Robson is a Lancashire lass. She was born in Wigan, in North England, December 13, 1880. Her mother is Madge Carr-Cooke, who made so real on the stage that celebrated American optimist, Mrs. Wiggs of the Cabbage Patch. Her father died when she was but five years old, and her mother brought her to America and placed her with the Sisters in St. Peter's Academy, Staten Island. When she graduated in 1897, she crossed the continent at once to join her mother, who was a member of the Frawley Stock Company at the California Theatre in San Francisco.

It was probably inevitable that this daughter of three generations of artists should have found herself most at home in the theatre. An accident, however, arranged her début for her. The day she arrived in San Francisco, the actress who was cast for Marguerite Knox in "Men and Women" was taken ill, and the young graduate promptly agreed to fill the breach. In two years she developed her talents in all sorts of parts in stock companies from Honolulu to Milwaukee before she really came into her own as Bonita, the ranchman's daughter, in Augustus Thomas's "Arizona." This was first produced at the Grand Opera House, Chicago, August 21, 1899. She revealed a rich beauty, a charmingly sympathetic personality, and rare sureness of technique for one so young. It was in this part that she made her New York debut at the Herald Square Theatre in the fall of 1900. Disappointed in his effort to secure Julia Marlowe for a performance of Browning's "In a Balcony" in conjunction with Otis Skinner and Mrs. LeMoyne, George C. Tyler, of Liebler & Co., gave the rôle of Constance to Miss Robson. From that time she has known no other management, and her lovely performance of Constance marked her for a conspicuous place among American artists.

After creating leading rôles in "Unleavened Bread," and "A Gentleman of France," she was starred in a dramatization of "Audrey," and thereafter in Zangwill's "Merely Mary Ann," Fitch's "The Girl Who Has Everything"; Jerome's "Susan in Search of a Husband"; Zangwill's "Nurse Marjorie"; Clo Graves's "A Tenement Tragedy"; Armstrong's "Salomy Jane," and Mrs. Burnett's "The Dawn of a To-morrow." In brief tours by "all-star casts" she has played Juliet and Kate Hardcastle. All she does is characterized by sincerity, grace, charm, tenderness, and humor.

Mr JAMES T POWERS

THE transit of James T. Powers from messenger boy to musical comedy star has been through a tea store; a minstrel troupe, which gave one performance in Mount Vernon, New York, after which he walked home; knockabout singing and dancing in a variety hall at Long Branch, New Jersey; the more polite vaudeville; small parts in farces and comic opera; two years in English theatres; and long New York engagements as leading comedian.

This chronicle extended reveals a steady growth in his own work through many varied experiences in well-remembered farces and comic operas which became popular largely owing to his excellent fun. After the minstrel and variety days Mr. Powers joined a stock company at the Eighth Street Theatre in New York, the town of his birth. A year here directed his talents, and he began to play parts in productions. In 1880 he was Chip with Willie Edouin in "Dreams, or Fun in a Photograph Gallery," then the Policeman in "Evangeline," and again with Edouin in "A Bunch of Keys." Edouin took him to London, where he played in "A Bunch of Keys," in several plays with the Vokes family, at the Empire in "Chilperic" and as the Emperor in "Dick Whittington," the Drury Lane Christmas pantomime of 1884.

He came home and played Rats in "A Tin Soldier"; principal comedy parts at the Casino in "Madelon," "Nadjy," "The Yeoman of the Guard," "The Drum Major," and "Erminie," and starred for four years in "A Straight Tip," "A Mad Bargain," "Walker, London," and "The New Boy," which were all farces.

For five years, from 1897 to 1902, he was leading comedian at Daly's Theatre in that popular series of imported English musical pieces which included "The Circus Girl," "The Geisha," "La Poupée," "A Runaway Girl," "San Toy," "The Messenger Boy," "The Jewel of Asia," and "The Princess of Kensington." His appearances since have been in "The Medal and the Maid," a term in vaudeville, and as a star in "The Blue Moon," and "Havana."

IN "THE NEW BOY"

IN "SAN TOY"

FLIPPER IN "A RUNAWAY GIRL."

IN "THE MESSENGER BOY"

IN "THE CIRCUS GIRL"

THERE is little that is extraordinary or romantic on the surface of Maclyn Arbuckle's career on the stage. It is the simple story of a man of genuine talent who had nursed it conscientiously and has risen little by little to a conspicuous place among sound actors in naturalistic comedy.

Mr. Arbuckle is a native of San Antonio, Texas, where he was born July 9, 1866. He studied in Glasgow, Scotland, and in Boston, and was admitted to the bar in Texarkana, Texas. During the first year as a lawyer, however, his opportunities to do other things than practise were rarely disturbed. He devoted his enforced leisure to the study of Shakespeare and became fired with a desire to go on the stage.

Every actor finds his way to the stage by a different route. Arbuckle pioneered his way somehow down in the northeast corner of Texas and finally made his first appearance on Christmas Day, 1888, with Pete Baker as a German in "The Emigrant." His succeeding engagement was more in harmony with his ambition, for he joined R. D. MacLean and for four years acted only Shakespearian rôles.

In 1892 Charles Frohman engaged him for three years for his touring companies, and Mr. Arbuckle followed this with a year in San Francisco in Frawley's stock company. Here he played many of W. H. Crane's most popular characters. A season as leading support of Louis James, during which he played Marc Antony in "Julius Cæsar," was followed by a tour in "The Man From Mexico." His fortunes at this point took a decided turn, for, in 1898, he went to London, where he played Smith, in "Why Smith Left Home," with great success.

A début as a star followed in December, 1900, when he appeared at the Republic (now the Belasco) Theatre in a dramatization of Mollie Elliott Sewell's "The Sprightly Romance of Marsac." Subsequent rôles were Rockingham in "Under Two Flags" with Blanche Bates, Antonio in Nat Goodwin's production of "The Merchant of Venice," Skipper in "Skipper & Co.," and Jim Hackler in George Ade's "The County Chairman." He starred four years in this comedy and followed it with his amusing characterizations of Slim Hoover, the fat man, in "The Round Up," and of Fighting Hime Look in "The Circus Man."

IN "WHY SMITH LEFT HOME"

IN "THE COUNTY CHAIRMAN"

IN "THE ROUND UP"

IN "THE CIRCUS MAN"

IN "TESS OF THE D'URBERVILLES"

MRS. FISKE
IN "MARY OF MAGDALA"

IN "MAGDA"

MINNIE MADDERN FISKE is an actress who discloses the mental process of the characters she portrays. It is not sufficient for her to show what they do and say and feel, she shows plainly their mental state and activity. This represents, however, an attainment of the third and longest period of an active and varied career, during which she has been a child actress, a popular girl star in sentimental domestic drama, and finally one of the most original and powerful emotional actresses of her time.

Minnie Maddern was born in New Orleans, December 19, 1865, of a manager father, Thomas W. Davey, and an actress mother, Lizzie Maddern. During the first ten years she was alternately at convent schools in the West and playing

IN "ROSMERSHOLM"

child parts of every description with E. L. Davenport, Mrs. Scott Siddons, "Fritz" Emmett, Barry Sullivan, Lucille Western and Junius Brutus Booth. She sang Ralph Rackstraw in Hooley's Juvenile Pinafore Company and created scores of parts before she became a star in her sixteenth year.

Her most popular pieces, as a youthful star, were "Fogg's Ferry," "Caprice" and "In Spite of All." In 1890 she married Harrison Grey Fiske and retired from the stage. Her reappearance as Minnie Maddern Fiske, four years later, revealed an actress whose art had individualized, no less than matured, and her list of productions and characterizations is one of the most inspiring pages in the history of the American stage.

It includes the vehicle of her return to the stage, "Hester Crewe," by her husband; Nora in "A Doll's House"; Gilberte in "Frou-Frou"; "The Queen of Liars," later reproduced as "Marie Deloche"; "Cesarine," an English version of "La Femme de Claude"; her own "A Light From St. Agnes"; Tess in "Tess of the D'Urbervilles"; Cyprienne in "Divorçons"; Saucers in "A Bit of Old Chelsea"; Madeleine in "Love Finds the Way"; "Magda"; Giulia in "Little Italy"; "Becky Sharp"; "Miranda of the Balcony"; "The Unwelcome Mrs. Hatch," "Mary of Magdala"; "Hedda Gabler"; "Leah Kleschna"; "Dolce"; Cynthia Karslake in "The New York Idea"; Rebecca West in "Rosmersholm"; and Nell Sanders in "Salvation Nell."

Mrs. Fiske has always been the presiding genius of any stage on which she has acted, directing all the details of her productions. She has written much and has made many public addresses. Her acted plays, in addition to "A Light From St. Agnes," include "The Rose," in which George Arliss acted with much success, "The Eyes of the Heart" and "Not Guilty." She has never sought a career abroad, but during long tours she has visited every city in the United States and Canada.

IN "MARY OF MAGDALA"

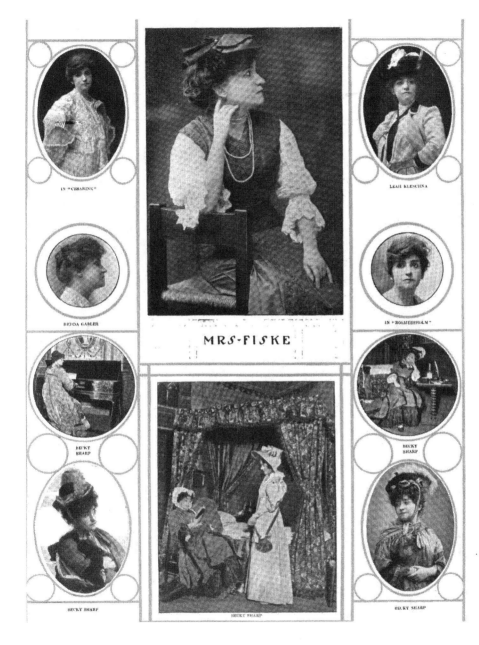

IN "THE MAN WHO OWNS BROADWAY"

IN "THE MAN WHO OWNS BROADWAY"

IN "THE YANKEE CONSUL"

IN "THE GALLOPER"

MR. RAYMOND HITCHCOCK

THERE are instances innumerable of comic opera comedians who have successfully entered straight comedy. Conspicuous examples are Richard Mansfield, W. H. Crane and Francis Wilson. There are instances of comedians who have abandoned drama for a career in comic opera. De Wolf Hopper is one of these. Raymond Hitchcock furnishes a composite instance of a facile character actor who has swung back and forth between the two branches of his profession.

Auburn, New York, was his birthplace. He began modestly as an amateur actor, but for his professional début he nursed a bold plan to play "Ingomar." The results were inevitable, and he thought them over behind a counter in Wanamaker's store in Philadelphia. His real footing on the stage was obtained in the chorus of the Carlton Opera Company when they were singing "The Brigand," in 1891. While the company was playing in Montreal, Charles Bigelow was ill and he had his first chance to play a part.

For twelve years Mr. Hitchcock played in comedies both with and without music. He played Sir Tobin Topax in "The Golden Wedding," a long list in the repertoire of the Castle Square Opera Company, Uncle Hank in the original production of "We Uns of Tennessee," David Tooke in "Three Little Lambs," in "The Belle of Bridgeport," "A Dangerous Maid," "Vienna Life," "The Burgomaster," "Miss Bob White," and "King Dodo."

He appeared first as a star in September, 1903, in the character of Abijah Booze in "The Yankee Consul," and sang "It Was Not Like This in the Olden Time." He went back to comedy in "Easy Dawson," and "The Galloper," into comic opera again in "The Student King," and has since been starred in a musical version of "The Galloper," called "The Yankee Tourist," in a revival of "The Mascot" and in "The Man Who Owns Broadway."

Miss MAY IRWIN

IN "SISTER MARY"
IN "MRS. BLACK IS BACK"
IN "A NIGHT OFF"

IT is perhaps truer of the people of the stage than of those of any other profession, that the beginning has no relation to the end. A career is an evolution, but the stages of the process often bear baffling relations to each other. May Irwin's career as a public entertainer had four almost wholly unrelated aspects. When she was eight years old, she sang soprano in a church choir. That was in Whitby, Ontario, where she was born in 1862. In those days there was no "polite vaudeville." This form of entertainment was given in what were known as "variety houses," and they were not regarded sympathetically by the church. Yet May Irwin's first step from the church choir was onto the stage of Daniel Shelby's Adelphi Variety Theatre in Buffalo, where she and her sister sang duets.

The Irwin Sisters sang in the variety theatres of the Middle West until Tony Pastor saw them in Detroit and brought them to his theatre in Fourteenth Street, New York. They remained there four years. By another of those unrelated transitions, May Irwin, in 1884, passed immediately from singing in the smoky unconventionality of Tony Pastor's to acting in Augustin Daly's exclusive patrician theatre on Broadway, where she was a valued actress of comedy servants. She was especially funny as Susan in "A Night Off" and Lucy in "The Recruiting Officer." She accompanied the Daly company on both their trips abroad.

When she left Daly's company there followed a detached interval during which she sang again in variety theatres, acted Helen Stockton in "The Junior Partner" with Henry Miller, Ophelia in "Poets and Puppets" under Charles Frohman, a leading part in Russell's "City Directory," and in support of Peter Dailey in "A Country Sport."

Miss Irwin has been a star in farce since 1895, when she produced "The Widow Jones." The list of succeeding pieces includes "The Swell Mrs. Fitzwell," "Courted into Court," "Kate Kip, Buyer," "Sister Mary," "The Belle of Bridgeport," "Madge Smith, Attorney," "Mrs. Black is Back," "Mrs. Wilson, That's All" and "Mrs. Peckham's Carouse." They were all written to fit her. But as her fun was all normal and natural, though carried to the highest power of laugh making, there was little in them that was extravagant.

Miss Irwin is acknowledged one of the greatest low comediennes of her time. To a gift for acting she disclosed in later years an almost wholly new side of her genius by her interpretation of "coon-songs."

IN "A ROYAL RIVAL."

ROMEO

"WILLIAM FAVERSHAM"

IN "THE SQUAW MAN"

WILLIAM FAVERSHAM'S recent adjustment of himself in a position among living actors of the first rank was prepared for during a long painstaking apprenticeship and, in its means, it affords a striking illustration of what can be accomplished by initiative based on independence. Mr. Faversham acted for other managers for a score of years. Three years ago he decided to be absolute master of his own artistic efforts and destinies. The result has been happy, not to say inspiring. His first production was "The World and His Wife," admirable from every point of view; and he has recently given the first American production of Stephen Phillips's "Herod" with real splendor.

Mr. Faversham was born February 17, 1868, in Warwickshire, England, and was educated in the Chigwell Grammar School, Essex, and at Hillmartin College. He "roughed it" in London and provincial companies for several years, at eighteen playing Hamlet at the St. James Theatre, Ramsgate, and came to New York in 1887. He made his début January 17th of that year at the Union Square Theatre in "Pen and Ink." The play failed, but Faversham made an impression, and Daniel Frohman engaged him for five years at the Lyceum.

He acted many parts with varying results during this association but won a distinct advance for himself by his Prince Emil von Haldenwald in Bronson Howard's "Aristocracy," at Palmer's, November 4, 1892. Charles Frohman engaged him for the Empire, and when he left that theatre at the end of nine years, he had been leading man for seven years of that term. At the Empire he played Simeon Brewster in "The Younger Son," Jack Medbury in "The Councillor's Wife," Ned Annesley in "Sowing the Wind," Reggie in "Gudgeons," Sir Brice Skene in "The Masqueraders," Sir Hubert Garlinge in "John A-Dreams," Algernon in "The Importance of Being Earnest," John Belton in "Marriage," Gil de Berault in "Under the Red Robe," Roger Ainslie in "A Man and His Wife," Eric in "The Conquerors," Lord Wheatley in "Phroso," Lord Algy in "Lord and Lady Algy," Romeo to Maude Adams's Juliet, Martin in "My Lady's Lord," John Hinds in "Brother Officers," and Henri Beauclerc in "Diplomacy."

His stellar début was made August 19, 1901, at the Criterion as Don Cæsar in "A Royal Rival" and he has since continued as a star as Jack Frere in "Imprudence," Captain Harry Peyton in "Miss Elizabeth's Prisoner," Richard Brinsley Sheridan in "Mr. Sheridan," as Neville Letchmere in "Letty," Jim Carston in "The Squaw Man," Don Ernesto in "The World and His Wife," and King Herod in "Herod."

MR. WILLIAM FAVERSHAM

DON ERNESTO IN "THE WORLD AND HIS WIFE"

KING HEROD

ROMEO

IN "THE SQUAW MAN"

IN "BROTHER OFFICERS"

IN "LORD AND LADY ALGY"

Miss MARGARET ANGLIN

ALTHOUGH Margaret Anglin has since achieved prominence by virtue of her skilfully developed native gifts she had a certain distinction thrust upon her at birth. Her father was at the time Speaker of the Canadian House, a post which carries with it the privilege of residence in the Parliament building at Ottawa, and here she was born. While at school in a French convent she began to disclose her dramatic talent and, when seventeen years old, she defied parental authority and went to New York to attend a dramatic school. She so pleased Mr. Frohman by her acting in one of the student performances that he cast her for the part of Madelaine West in Bronson Howard's "Shenandoah," and she made her professional début in this play at the Academy of Music in the fall of 1894.

Since then she has climbed steadily upward to a secure position in the front rank of her profession, where she is distinguished not only as a gifted actress but as her own manager. The rôles by which she has come into her present prominence are varied and interesting. In 1896 her second engagement promoted her to the position of leading woman to James O'Neil, with whom she played Ophelia, Virginia, Mercedes in "Monte Cristo," and Julie de Mortimer in "Richelieu," and then she made so bold as to organize her own company and to tour Lower Canada as a star.

Now began the chain of significant events in her career. Engaged for minor parts with E. H. Sothern, she one night had a chance to play Lady Ursula, as a result of which her next opportunity was to create Roxane in Mansfield's production of "Cyrano de Bergerac." Her noble and beautiful performance of this character at once established her as an able artist. This was followed in the autumn by her creation of Constance in "The Musketeers," Heloise in "Citizen Pierre," and of Mimi in "The Only Way."

In 1900 she became leading woman of the Empire Company, a post she retained till the company finally disbanded. She appeared in "Brother Officers," "The Bugle Call," "Mrs. Dane's Defense," "Diplomacy," "The Wilderness," "The Twin Sister," "The Importance of Being Earnest," and "The Unforeseen." About this time she earned popularity in San Francisco as joint stock star with Henry Miller. Out of this association grew her secure position as one of America's leading stars. In 1905 she came to the unfortunate little up-stairs Princess Theatre in "Zira" and great was her success, which she further accented a year later on the same stage by her triumph as Ruth Jordan in "The Great Divide." Equally notable is her latest creation, Helena in "The Awakening of Helena Richie," under her own management. Miss Anglin spent the year 1908 in Australia and won hearty recognition for her performances in "The Thief," "The Taming of the Shrew," "Zira," and as Viola in "Twelfth Night."

CATHERINE IN "THE TAMING OF THE SHREW" AND VIOLA IN "TWELFTH NIGHT"

IN "THE AWAKENING OF HELENA RICHIE"

IN "THE GREAT DIVIDE"

IN "ZIRA"

Miss MARGARET ANGLIN

IN "THE THIEF"
Copyright Talma Studios

MR DE WOLF HOPPER

IN "THE LADY OR THE TIGER"

IN "EL CAPITAN"

IN "THE BLACK HUSSAR"

WILLIAM DE WOLF HOPPER is a descendant of the De Wolfs of Providence on his maternal line, and his father's family were Philadelphia Quakers. The first plan for his future was that he should follow his father's profession and become a lawyer. Amateur theatricals developed another talent, however, and he decided to be an actor.

There are many roads to the stage, but Hopper, at twenty-one, had fifty thousand dollars and he made his début as backer or "angel" and as actor at the same time. The first play he produced was "Our Boys" and he acted Talbot Champneys. This was in 1878. The last copper of his bank account went into the next venture, which exploited Ada Gilman as a star in a Mormon melodrama, "The Hundred Wives." Georgie Drew Barrymore was in the cast. The next time he acted he was paid for it by Harrigan and Hart, and the play was "The Blackbird."

At the suggestion of Clara Louise Kellogg he studied singing with a view to a grand opera career, but he continued to act in various productions while studying, until Col. McCaull engaged him for his celebrated opera company, and he seized a chance opportunity in Philadelphia to understudy one of the principals and he made a hit as Pomeret in "Desiret." He became first comedian at once. He maintained himself in the position with increasing popularity for five years from 1885 to 1890, when he took his place at the head of his own company. Mr. Hopper has ranked from the first as one of the most legitimately funny of all comic comedians and the superior of any as a singer.

With the McCaull company he played the leading rôles in "The Black Hussar," "The Beggar Student," "Die Fledermaus," "The Lady or the Tiger," "Loraine," "The Bellman," "Josephine Sold by Her Sisters," "Falka," "Chatter," "Boccaccio," "Jacquette," "Prince Methusalem," "Clover," and "The Begum." As a star his operas have been: "Castles in the Air," "Wang," "Panjandrum," "Dr. Syntax," "El Capitan," "The Charlatan," "Mr. Pickwick," "Happyland," "The Pied Piper," and "The Matinée Idol." When The Lambs gamboled on tour, in 1909, one of the features of their striking entertainment was Mr. Hopper's appearance as Marc Antony in the Forum scene from Shakespeare's "Julius Cæsar."

Inseparably associated with Mr. Hopper is the baseball epic, "Casey at the Bat." He recited it first in 1885. The two teams playing in New York were to make a baseball night at Wallack's Theatre while he was playing there. That very day Archibald Clavering Gunter had read "Casey" in a San Francisco paper and cut it out, and it was suggested that Hopper recite it from the stage. It was a hit from the first and Mr. Hopper has spent the balance of his career fighting the demands of audiences for those verses. For years he sought the identity of the author behind the initials "E. L. T." on the original copy. One night, when playing at Worcester, Massachusetts, he was invited to meet the author of "Casey," and discovered him to be Ernest L. Thayer, a manufacturer of that city.

IN "THE PIED PIPER" Photograph by Hall

MISS ISABEL IRVING

ISABEL IRVING has been acting important parts in the leading theatres since she first went on the stage. She made her début, when fifteen years old, without any previous experience or preparation, in Rosina Vokes's delightful little comedy company, at the Standard Theatre, New York City, December 7, 1886, playing Gwendoline in "The Schoolmistress." She remained with Miss Vokes almost continuously for two years.

Augustin Daly became impressed by her beauty and talent, and her third season on the stage began as a member of his company. She played a varied round of modern, romantic and Shakespearian comedy parts for five seasons, acting with the Daly Company in London and Paris. At the Vaudeville Theatre in the French capital, she played Ada Rehan's part, Jo, in "The Lottery of Love." Some of the parts she played during this time were Caroline in "Needles and Pins," Jenny in "An International Match," Pansy in "The Great Unknown," Audrey in "As You Like It," Suzette in "A Priceless Paragon," Faith Rutherell in "The Last Word," Virginia in the pantomime "The Prodigal Son," Katherine in "Love's Labor's Lost," Imogene in "The Cabinet Minister," Daisy Griffing in "Nancy & Co.," Sabina in "A Test Case," Helen in "The Hunchback," Susan in "A Night Off," and Oberon in "A Midsummer Night's Dream."

From Daly's she went in 1894 to the other principal New York company, that at the Lyceum Theatre, where she played leading parts in the productions of "The Amazons," "A Woman's Silence," "The Case of Rebellious Susan," "An Ideal Husband," "Fortune," "The Home Secretary," "The Benefit of the Doubt," and the revival of "The Prisoner of Zenda." She was John Drew's leading woman in his performances of "A Marriage of Convenience," "The Liars," "The Tyranny of Tears," and "One Summer's Day."

Since 1901 she has appeared in "To Have and to Hold," with Blanche Bates in "Under Two Flags," with Charles Hawtrey in "A Message from Mars," with Faversham in "A Royal Rival," as Constance Neville in the all-star revival of "She Stoops to Conquer," and as a star she has toured in "The Crisis," "The Toast of the Town," "Susan in Search of a Husband," and "The Girl Who Has Everything." During the season of 1909, she played the leading part in "The Commanding Officer."

AS THE LEECH IN "TOM JONES"

IN "IN THE PALACE OF THE KING"

IN "BABES IN TOYLAND"

BARRY IN "THE COUNTRY GIRL"

Mr William NORRIS

PEPE THE JESTER IN "FRANCESCA DA RIMINI"

WILLIAM NORRIS, during not quite twenty years on the stage, has distinguished himself in nearly every form of theatrical entertainment. He was born in San Francisco. After his school days there, during which he often appeared in amateur performances, he came to New York and made his first professional appearance when twenty-one years old in "The Girl from Mexico" at the Standard Theatre, December 21, 1891. His first real success, however, was made in support of Marie Jansen two years later in "Delmonico's at Six" and "Miss Dynamite."

Richard Mansfield engaged him for his Garrick Theatre Company when he opened that little playhouse, and Mr. Norris created rôles there in "A Man With a Past," "A Social Highwayman," and "The Thoroughbred." When Warfield gave up the part of the Polite Lunatic in "The Belle of New York," Mr. Norris took it up and made it as amusing and distinctive a feature of this piece as Dan Daly's Mr. Bronson. Less effective were his efforts in "A Normandy Wedding" and "A Dangerous Maid," but his creation of Baverstock, the secretary, in "His Excellency the Governor," Pinchas, the little poet of the Ghetto, in Zangwill's "Children of the Ghetto," the dwarf jester in Crawford's "In the Palace of the King," with Viola Allen; and Pepe, the jester, in Otis Skinner's revival of "Francesca da Rimini," were four strongly characterized portraits worthy of the highest standards in character acting.

Since that time, Mr. Norris has made two appearances as a dramatic star. His first essay was as the Yiddish clothing merchant, Pincus Mayer, in "The Business Man" at McVicker's Theatre, Chicago, in 1903, and in 1906 as Clarence Chope in "Sir Anthony" at the Savoy Theatre, New York.

His other important characterizations have been in leading parts in musical comedy productions, where he has displayed other phases of the same talents which he employed in drama without music. His well remembered parts have been Alan in "Babes in Toyland," The Man in the Moon in "The Land of Nod," Peter Stuyvesant in "The Burgomaster," Chambhuddy Ram in "The Cingalee," Barry in "The Country Girl," the title rôle in "King Dodo," Benjamin Partridge, the leech, in "Tom Jones," and the leading part in "The King of Cadonia."

JOCELYN

CARMEN

MISS ROSE COGHLAN
IN "JACK STRAW"

PENELOPE IN "ULYSSES"

LADY TEAZLE

AMONG the finest performances of emotional rôles and of that line of parts which are conventionally termed "adventuresses" which the American theatre has known are those which have been given by Rose Coghlan. She was born in Peterborough, England, and her father was Francis Coghlan, publisher of Coghlan's Continental Guides, and a friend of Dickens. Charles Coghlan was her brother.

Her first appearance on the stage was made in Greenwich, Scotland, as one of the witches in "Macbeth." Soon she was playing in London in support of Adelaide Neilson and J. E. Toole. When she was nineteen years old E. H. Sothern brought her to America, in 1872, and her first appearances here were made at Wallack's Theatre, in September of that year, as Mrs. Honeyton in the comedy of "A Happy Pair" and as Jupiter in F. C. Burnand's extravaganza "Ixion." With Sothern she acted in the trinity of Dundreary comedies: "Our American Cousin," "Brother Sam," and "Dundreary Married and Settled." Four years followed in England, during which time she played with Charles Mathews, Joseph Jefferson and Barry Sullivan; toured the Provinces in "A School for Scandal," "Twelfth Night," and "East Lynne," and created Lady Manden in "All For Her" and acted it for four hundred nights at the St. James Theatre.

Miss Coghlan returned to America in 1877 and for eleven years she was almost continuously the leading woman at Wallack's Theatre, and such was her popularity that the plays were selected largely with a view to her largest opportunity. Among her great performances were Magdalen in "False Shame," Countess Zicka in Sardou's "Diplomacy," Clarissa in "Clarissa Harlowe," "Camille," Stephanie in "Forget-me-not," "Le Belle Russe," Lady Teazle in "The School for Scandal," Peg Woffington in "Masks and Faces," Vere Herbert in "Moths," Nellie Denver in "The Silver King," and Lady Gay Spanker in "London Assurance." When the celebrated cast was assembled to play "Hamlet" on Lester Wallack's retirement from the stage, May 21, 1888, Miss Coghlan acted The Player Queen.

Mr. Wallack's retirement disbanded his famous company and Miss Coghlan became a star at the head of her own company. Her most popular plays were "Our Joan," "Princess Olga," "Lady Barter," "A Woman of No Importance," "Peg Woffington," "Nance Oldfield," "Jocelyn" and "Madame," the last two written for her by her brother. More recently she has only accepted occasional engagements when the rôles have been congenial. She created parts in the American productions of "The White Heather," "Mlle. Fi-Fi," "Ulysses," "The Duke of Killicrankie" and "Jack Straw." Miss Coghlan is a member of the New Theatre company.

MISS ROSE COGHLAN

Mr E M HOLLAND

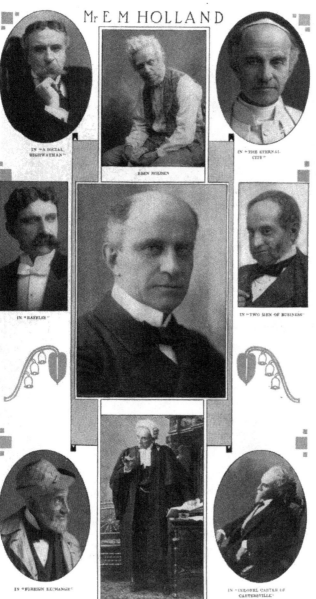

THERE'S many an actor who cannot star and there is many a star who cannot act. Edmund M. Holland falls more really within the lines of the former classification. For if he cannot star all the time, the time has not been when he could not act.

He made his début on the stage in 1855 as a youngster in "To Parents and Guardians" at Wallack's Lyceum Theatre; and many interesting and diversified experiences were compressed into his early years, including three years as call boy at Mrs. Wood's Olympic Theatre, small parts at Barnum's Museum, and a part in the cast which surrounded Joseph Jefferson the first time he played "Rip Van Winkle" in New York.

He came from a family of actors but he brought the name Holland into new casts only when he joined Lester Wallack's company in 1867, for during his early years on the stage he was known by only a portion of his full name, Edmund Milton. After thirteen consecutive seasons with Mr. Wallack he went to A. M. Palmer at his Union Square Theatre and, after several changes, once more found a permanent home in Mr. Palmer's company, first at the Madison Square Theatre and later at Palmer's. He remained with Mr. Palmer thirteen years, giving performances which are historic. Among them were Captain Redwood in "Jim the Penman," Mr. Gardiner in "Captain Swift," Berkley Brue in "Aunt Jack," Gregory in "A Pair of Spectacles," Lot Burden in "Saints and Sinners," Colonel Moberley in "Alabama," and the Colonel in "Colonel Carter of Cartersville."

Richard Mansfield presented E. M. Holland and his brother Joseph Holland at his Garrick Theatre in 1895 in "A Man With a Past," and then starred them in "A Social Highwayman" for two years. Mr. Holland has created many splendid characters during the last dozen years. His best remembered parts are, perhaps, the Pope in "The Eternal City," Captain Bedford in "Raffles," Gentle in "The Battle," Eben Holden in the play of that name, and Bates in "The House of a Thousand Candles." In the last two plays he was again a star. In December, 1909, Mr. Holland created Mr. Baxter in "Foreign Exchange," then became a member of the New Theatre company, making his first appearance as Sir Oliver in "The School for Scandal."

MISS HEDWIG REICHER

IN "ON THE EVE" SALOME

THE latest of the foreign-born, foreign-tongued actresses to learn English with a view to an American career is Hedwig Reicher. She is a very young woman, and, as her name suggests, came from Germany.

Miss Reicher is the daughter of Emmanuel Reicher, himself one of the leading actors of Germany and the first to stage and to act the plays of Ibsen in his own country. Her mother was Lena Harf, for many years the principal actress of the Lessing Theatre in Berlin. In her Berlin home Miss Reicher grew up under the influence of the studious and artistic atmosphere created by her parents and their associates. Ibsen was often a guest there for long visits.

She made her début when sixteen in the leading rôle of Hermann Bahr's play, "The Housewife," at Hamburg, where her father had taken the theatre for the summer, and she acted continuously while her father remained. But she did not follow up a career on the stage uninterruptedly. There were months of retirement and study at home between engagements with stock companies with whom her father appeared as a star. His repertoire was made up largely of plays by Shakespeare, Hauptmann, Ibsen, Lessing, and Strindberg. She acted the principal women.

The first time Miss Reicher tasted the real sweets of triumph was for her performance of Hoffmanstahl's "Electra" at Aix-la-Chapelle. That gave her a secure position among the young leading women in Germany and she acted with the first companies of Leipsic and Berlin. She added to her repertoire notable performances of "Judith," "Frou-Frou," Nora in "A Doll's House," Moricka in "The Fires of St. John," and "Salome."

In 1907 she was engaged by the Director of the Municipal Theatre at Frankfort to become leading woman. Her engagement was to begin in the fall of 1908. This left her an interval of a year. About this time an offer came for her to play leading parts at the Irving Place Theatre, in New York, and she accepted with the dual thought of becoming acquainted with the new world and of seeing again her brother, Franz Reicher, who has been acting here in English in Mr. Sothern's and other leading companies for a dozen years.

Miss Reicher delighted her German audiences in New York. She was offered the leading rôles at the New German Theatre for the following year, and she canceled her contract in Frankfort and remained. Her performances attracted widespread attention, and Henry B. Harris, in April, 1909, offered to star her in September of the same year if she would learn English. She consented and "On the Eve" was chosen for her début. With her brother she retired to the mountains to study the new language of which she knew not a word. Her début was personally successful in spite of the version of the play. Her second English rôle was Paula Marsh in Charles Klein's "Next of Kin."

IN "TWIRLY WHIRLY"

MISS
LILLIAN
RUSSELL

IN "HOITY TOITY"

IN "WILDFIRE"

Photograph by Hall

ONE evening in a theatrical boarding-house, near his old theatre in Broadway opposite Niblo's Garden, Tony Pastor heard a girl's voice which charmed him so that he offered her fifty dollars a week to sing ballads in his theatre. That was in 1879. Her name was Helen Louise Leonard. Mr. Pastor renamed her Lillian Russell, under which name she long reigned as the most beautiful and attractive woman on the American comic opera stage.

She was born eighteen years before in Clinton, Iowa, where her father was an editor and her mother a woman's rights advocate. She went to school in the Sacred Heart Convent, Chicago, and studied singing with Madame Jovinaily and later in New York under Dr. Leopold Damrosch. For the sake of stage experience she joined the chorus of E. E. Rice's "H. M. S. Pinafore" company when eighteen, but retired within two months.

Her next appearance was as Lillian Russell at Tony Pastor's, where she established herself at once and permanently in public affection. Tours in concert and opera as far as the Pacific Coast followed. In 1883 she became prima donna of the Casino. Her first rôle in this house was Constance in "The Sorcerer." In the summer of that year she went to England, where she appeared in "Virginia and Paul" and in "Polly," two operas written for her by Edward Solomon.

Resuming her career in New York, she was in demand for the production of every new opera and seldom appeared twice in succession in the same theatre until she returned to the Casino in 1889, where she remained two years. In one theatre and another during this period and until she returned to London she was the original in America in "Polly," Virginia in "The Maid and the Moonshiner," "Dorothy," Inez in "The Queen's Mate," Princess Etelka in "Nadjy," Fiorella in "The Brigands," "The Grand Duchess," Harriet in "Poor Jonathan," Pythia in "Apollo," Marton in "La Cigale," Teresa in "The Mountebanks," the twin sisters in "Giroflé-Girofla" and Rosa in "The Princess Nicotine."

Miss Russell's second visit to London was made as a star. She produced "The Queen of the Brilliants" at Henry Irving's Lyceum Theatre, September 8, 1894, with but little success. Two months later she appeared in the same opera at Abbey's (now the Knickerbocker) Theatre and during the six years succeeding sang the prima donna rôles in "La Perichole," "La Tzigane," "The Goddess of Truth," "An American Beauty," "The Wedding Day," "La Belle Hélène" and "Erminie." The next four years she spent at Weber and Fields's Music Hall, and then resumed her place at the head of her own company, singing "Lady Teazle" in an operatic version of Sheridan's comedy, "The School for Scandal." In 1906 she began to act in plays without music and has since toured in "Barbara's Millions," "Wildfire," "The Widow's Might," and "The First Night."

MISS LILLIAN RUSSELL

MR LOUIS JAMES

CARDINAL WOLSEY IN "KING HENRY VIII"

RICHARD III

FEW living actors have equaled Louis James in the variety of their experience and the importance of their achievement. None who is conspicuous on the stage to-day reaches so far back. Forty years ago he was one of the leading young artists of the American theatre. He has embellished his long career with many fine achievements; for twenty-five years he has starred in Shakespeare, and he survives as one of our three leading living Shakespearian actors.

Mr. James was born in Freeport, Illinois, in 1841. He went on the stage in 1863 in the company at Macauley's Theatre, Louisville. For six years he was one of the leading players of Mrs. John Drew's celebrated company at the Arch Street Theatre, Philadelphia, and in 1871 he took a prominent place in Augustin Daly's company which he held by virtue of fine achievements for five years. He acted Captain Lynde in "Divorce," Henry Delile in "Article 47," Doricourt in "The Belle's Stratagem," Master Page in "The Merry Wives of Windsor," Joseph Surface in "The School for Scandal," Major Whist in "Saratoga," Longaville in "Love's Labor's Lost," Bill Sykes in "Oliver Twist," young Marlow in "She Stoops to Conquer," and Master Heywood in "Yorick's Love." He was the first to act several of these parts.

After playing leading parts in McVicker's company in Chicago, and Maguire's in San Francisco, he was leading support for Lawrence Barrett for five years. In 1885 he began to star with Marie Wainwright and played "Virginius," "Othello," "Ingomar," "The Love Chase," "Much Ado About Nothing," and other standard and classical plays.

Since 1889 Mr. James has starred alone except when special productions have been made and Modjeska, Frederick Warde or Katherine Kidder have co-starred with him. He has presented nearly every play in the Shakespearian repertoire, showing equal facility as Hamlet or Bottom, Macbeth or Orlando, Othello or Caliban, Shylock or a Dromio, Wolsey or Benedick.

In the all-star revival of "The Two Orphans," first given at the New Amsterdam Theatre in 1905, he was the Jacques Fouchard on tour, and later, in a similarly notable cast of "She Stoops to Conquer," he played Hardcastle to the Kate of Eleanor Robson and the young Marlow of Kyrle Bellew.

JASON GREEN
IN "OLD INNOCENCE"

JIM JOHNSTONE IN "A CORNER IN COFFEE"

MR TIM MURPHY

MAVERICK BRANDER
IN "A TEXAS STEER"

GOVERNOR CRANCK IN
"THE CARPET BAGGER"

DAVID HOLMES IN "A
BACHELOR'S ROMANCE"

TIM MURPHY is an actor of wide popularity throughout the United States who has made himself admired by the portrayal of quaint, amiable, and shrewd American types. He has a faculty amounting almost to genius for keeping his characters close to nature and he lightens them with a whimsical sense of humor. He is most often compared to John T. Raymond and Sol Smith Russell, and he is generally accredited an able exponent of the school of which Joseph Jefferson was the master.

Mr. Murphy was born on the eastern edge of New York state, but very early in life he moved with his parents to Washington, District of Columbia. As a boy he often acted in school and other amateur entertainments and eventually he was admitted to the Barrett Dramatic Club of which many well-known actors were graduates.

Charles H. Hoyt's farcical caricatures of American life caught his attention and he applied to the author-manager at the Madison Square Theatre. Mr. Hoyt gave him the character of Dodge Work in "A Brass Monkey" and was so much struck with his creation that he wrote for him the rôle of the Hon. Maverick Brander in "A Texas Steer."

After a long run in New York Mr. Murphy bought "A Texas Steer" and starred in it throughout America. Since that time he has been his own manager and has produced a new play and created a new rôle on an average of once a year. A glance down the list of Mr. Murphy's repertoire reveals the interesting fact that he has not played any other than American characters, unless exception be made of his admired imitation of Sir Henry Irving's Mathias in "The Bells" which he has used to round out an evening in connection with other plays. His most popular characterizations have been the Governor of Mississippi in Opie Read and Frank Pixley's "The Carpet Bagger"; Jason Green in "Old Innocence," from the same French source ("Les Petits Oiseaux") that Sydney Grundy took "A Pair of Spectacles"; David Holmes in Martha Morton's "A Bachelor's Romance"; Joel Gay in "A Capitol Comedy"; Jim Johnstone in the dramatization of the Rev. Cyrus Townsend Brady's "A Corner in Coffee"; John Crosby in Frederick Paulding's "Two Men and a Girl"; David Stratton in Charles Jeffrey's "Cupid and the Dollar"; and John Boland in Rupert Hughes's "My Boy."

MISS DORIS KEANE

DORIS KEANE is one of the young actresses who have come out of the West brimming with a temperament which is not usually associated with the native American nature. She was born in Michigan. Her parents moved to Chicago when she was a mere child, and she spent the earlier years of her life there. Her cosmopolitan experiences were enlarged by her schooling in New York and in European cities. When she decided upon the stage as a profession, she entered the American Academy of Dramatic Arts and took the course in acting, appearing in several public performances given by the students.

Miss Keane made her first professional appearance in the part of Rosie in Henry Arthur Jones's play, "Whitewashing Julia," at the Garrick Theatre, December 2, 1903. Mr. Frohman had selected her for this rôle, and she has not since acted under any other manager save for one summer, when she played in a stock company. He sent her on tour for her second year's experience to play in Augustus Thomas's "The Other Girl" in support of Lionel Barrymore, and in 1905 she was given the part of Irene Millard, the florist's daughter, in another of Mr. Thomas's plays, "De Lancey," in which John Drew starred.

Feeling the limitations of the one-part-a-year method to which modern methods often restrict a rising and ambitious actress, Miss Keane joined a summer stock company in St. Paul in 1906, and after only three years on the stage she acted all the leading rôles in this organization's repertoire. When she returned to New York in the autumn, Mr. Frohman cast her for the rôle in which she had her most brilliant opportunity, and she rose to the high level of the performance of those about her. This was in Henry Arthur Jones's "The Hypocrites" and her character was Rachel Neve. When Mr. Frohman produced this play at Hicks's Theatre, in London, the following year, he sent Miss Keane across the ocean to play the part she had originated.

In the spring of 1909, on April 12, at the Garrick Theatre, she created Joan Thornton, the leading part in "The Happy Marriage," by Clyde Fitch, and the last play which he lived to direct in its production. Miss Keane by this performance intensified the impression she had made in previous efforts. In the August following, at the Lyceum Theatre, she played Sonia Kritchnofe in the first production in English of Croisset and Leblanc's "Arsene Lupin."

MISS DORIS KEANE

LANCIOTTO IN "FRANCESCA DA RIMINI"

IN "THE HARVESTER"

SHYLOCK IN "THE MERCHANT OF VENICE"

IN "THE HARVESTER"

IN "THE DUEL."

Mr OTIS SKINNER

OTIS SKINNER is an artist of notable versatility on a high plane. His natural gifts are a keen intellect, plastic temperament, high spirits, gracious personality, lofty ideals, ambition, energy and zeal. His dramatic art is solidly founded on his experience as a young man in prominent parts in the companies of Edwin Booth, Lawrence Barrett, Helena Modjeska and Augustin Daly.

Mr. Skinner is the son of a Massachusetts clergyman, and was born in Cambridge, June 28, 1858. He adopted the stage as his profession before he was twenty, having made his début in a negro part, Plantation Jim, in "Woodleigh" at the Philadelphia Museum, in November, 1877. He acted in Philadelphia for two years before he came to New York, and very soon attracted the attention of Edwin Booth and Lawrence Barrett, in whose support he played for several years. His performance of Paolo in "Francesca da Rimini" to the Lanciotto of Lawrence Barrett established him as a young man of fine accomplishment and large promise, which he has not disappointed.

Augustin Daly engaged Skinner for his theatre and he maintained this association in America and England for four years, adding to his classic repertoire a list of light, modern and romantic rôles. In 1899 he was leading man for the Booth-Modjeska company. The next year he went to London, where, at the Globe, he played Romeo, and Percy Gauntlett in "This Woman and That." On his return to America, he became Helena Modjeska's principal support, playing Orlando, King Henry VIII, Sir Edward Mortimer in "Mary Stuart," Leonatus in "Cymbeline," Shylock in "The Merchant of Venice," Benedick in "Much Ado About Nothing," and Major Schubert in "Magda." He next added Captain Absolute to his list, in support of Joseph Jefferson in "The Rivals."

Save for one year, during which he starred jointly with Ada Rehan, playing Charles Surface, Petruchio and Shylock, he has been an independent star ever since. The list of characters and plays which Skinner has produced includes "His Grace de Grammont," "The King's Jester," "Villon the Vagabond," "A Soldier of Fortune," "Prince Rudolph," "The Liars," "Hamlet," "King Richard III," "Rosemary," "Prince Otto," "In a Balcony," Lanciotto in "Francesca da Rimini," "Lazarre," "The Harvester," the Abbé Daniel in "The Duel," Colonel Bridau in "The Honor of the Family," and La Fayette Towers in Booth Tarkington and Harry Leon Wilson's "Your Humble Servant."

MR OTIS SKINNER

IN "THE NAUTCH DANCE"

ANY record of the stage in America to-day would not be representative of the varied forms of artistic eloquence which does not include reference to the young American dancer, Ruth St. Denis. Her story is brief, for she is new in the public eye, but it is picturesque and significant.

Miss St. Denis was born on a New Jersey farm of an inventor father and a literary mother. Her first appearance before an audience was made in an amateur performance of "The Old Homestead" given in the district school house. In the play she acted Whistling Joe and between the acts she gave some movements which were called Exercises in Delsarte, but which she describes as "a thin attenuation of lessons received from a pupil of a pupil of Delsarte."

The next step was on to the professional stage and into one of Mr. Belasco's companies. But her capacity for acting seemed to hold little hope for her. One day there came to her the inspiration for the original excursions which were later to bring her fame. She says it was found in the figure of an Egyptian Deity which she saw exposed in a Buffalo shop window to advertise cigarettes. Forthwith she formed the plan of expressing through movement the religion and customs of the Orient.

In developing her idea and its setting the young woman, with her mother's assistance, studied the literature and art of the East, learned from Indians whom she sought out and lived with, and, when it came to giving form to her idea, so poor was she that she made her own costumes and painted much of her own scenery. No manager would venture her an opportunity to give her performance until a group of New York women subscribed enough to eliminate the possibility of loss.

She finally appeared at a special matinee at the Hudson Theatre and it at once became evident that an artist had arrived with a new idea to express. From New York Miss St. Denis went to the Aldwych Theatre, London, and to various European capitals. Her return to New York for the season of 1909 and 1910 has resulted in a veritable triumph.

Miss St. Denis's performance is more and less than dancing as conventionally known on our stage, since dancing generally means movement to rhythm, whereas in expressing her ideas she does not always confine the movement to the bounds either of rhythm or of music.

IN "THE USURPER"

IN "THE DEVIL"

IN "THE LION AND THE MOUSE"

JAQUELINE

MISS GRACE ELLISTON

GRACE ELLISTON is a leading woman who has rarely acted for any extended period far away from New York during recent years. She has created important parts in many productions, appearing in support of the most conspicuous stars, and during the winter of 1909 she made her own début as a star.

Miss Elliston is a West Virginia girl. The death of her father left it incumbent on her to contribute to the support of the family and she turned to the theatre as a hopeful opportunity. Her first engagements were in musical comedy, but her ambitions rose above this and her talents justified her ambitions.

She applied to Daniel Frohman who at that time still had his Lyceum Theatre on Fourth Avenue near Twenty-Third Street, known as "the parlor home of comedy," and he placed her in the cast of "Americans at Home," in which she played Dorothy, March 13, 1899. The same spring she played Ethel Carlton in "His Excellency the Governor" at the same theatre. The next autumn she was found in John Drew's support in "The Tyranny of Tears" at the Empire. In December at Hoyt's, known before and later as the Madison Square she acted Lady Curtoys in "Wheels Within Wheels"; and on February 5th following she was seen at Daly's as Alice Gainsborough in "The Ambassador." It was a busy and successful year for a novice in the drama and it raised Miss Elliston to a conspicuous position among the young actresses.

Soon after this she joined Henry Miller and acted during three summers in his splendid stock company in San Francisco, playing many and varied parts. She returned to New York with him in March, 1903, and appeared at the Savoy Theatre in Richard Harding Davis's comedy, "The Taming of Helen." That autumn Richard Mansfield produced "Old Heidelberg" and Miss Elliston created Kathie in this play on the night the Lyric Theatre was first opened to the public. She has since played Olivia in "Twelfth Night" with Viola Allen, the leading woman's part in "The Usurper" with N. C. Goodwin, Mildred in Robert Browning's "The Blot i' the 'Scutcheon" with Mrs. Le Moyne, Shirley Rossmore in Charles Klein's "The Lion and the Mouse" at the Lyceum Theatre in the autumn of 1905, Colombe in Browning's "Colombe's Birthday," Lady Gerania in "Dr. Wake's Patient," and made her début as a star at Worcester, Mass., November 29, 1909, in the title rôle of "Jaqueline."

THERE are difficulties in the way of being a Barrymore and not being an actor. They are hereditary and instinctive, a n d the American public is glad of it. The youngest of the family, John Barrymore, worked hard to surmount these difficulties. He had developed a talent as artist and illustrator and the possibilities of a successful career in this profession had opened to him when he succumbed to the call of the theatre.

Mr. Barrymore is a juvenile light comedian and a character actor of ability. He has advanced himself in the past seven years to what is professionally known as a "featured" position and it now seems inevitable that his sister Ethel will not long be the only one of their distinguished name who is a star in the theatrical firmament.

His début on the stage was made as Max in support of Nance O'Neil in "Magda," in Cleveland's Theatre, Chicago, October 31, 1903. Two months later he made his first appearance in New York, acting at the Savoy Theatre in "Glad Of It," and during the April following he appeared in William Collier's support at the Criterion Theatre as the telegraph operator in "The Dictator," playing the same character in London in the spring of 1905.

When he returned home he joined his sister's company and with her he acted Jackey in "Sunday," Stephen Rollo in "Alice Sit-by-the-Fire," and the clown in "Pantaloon." When Mr. Collier went to Australia in 1906 Mr. Barrymore accompanied him to play his original character in "The Dictator." On his return he rejoined his sister and later he succeeded Arnold Daly in the leading rôle of "The Boys of Company B" at the Lyceum Theatre and on tour. Charles Frohman cast him for Lord Meadows in "Toodles" and that brief experience was followed by an excursion into musical comedy, at first in Chicago as the Prince in "The Stubborn Cinderella" and later at the Knickerbocker in one of the leading parts in "The Candy Shop." His latest and most successful effort is as the hero in Winchell Smith's comedy without music, "The Fortune Hunter."

IN "THE FORTUNE HUNTER"

MR. JOHN BARRYMORE

MISS BLANCHE BATES

IN "THE FIGHTING HOPE."

BLANCHE BATES learned the rudiments of her art and laid the foundation for future success in the hard, hard work of stock acting on her native Pacific slope. Her father was the manager of a theatre in Portland, Oregon, and she was born in that city in 1873. Three years later the family moved to San Francisco, where she attended school.

Brander Matthews's one act play, "This Picture and That," was the vehicle for her first public appearance, when it was given at a benefit performance in San Francisco in 1894. Joining the T. D. Frawley stock company she was given utility parts. Her next step was into prominent rôles with the Giffin and Neill company, which played long seasons in Denver, Salt Lake City, San Francisco, and Portland, with a final week each year in Honolulu. Within a little over twelve months after adopting the stage she was playing leading characters in a wide variety of comedies and emotional plays.

Augustin Daly engaged Miss Bates in 1897 and she made her first New York appearance in his theatre in the autumn of that year as Bianca in "The Taming of the Shrew" and continued to play parts second to Ada Rehan's. When "The Great Ruby" was produced at Daly's she acted the Countess Mirtza twice and left the company. Although there was much printed comment on this incident, no explanation reached the public ear. In March, 1899, she played Miladi with James O'Neil in "The Musketeers" at the Broadway Theatre and Hannah in Zangwill's "Children of the Ghetto" at the Herald Square in October.

Miss Bates next appeared under David Belasco's management in "Naughty Anthony" with inconsiderable effect compared with that produced by her next creation as Cho-Cho-San in John Luther Long's "Madame Butterfly." After an interval with Chas. Frohman as Cigarette in a dramatization of Ouida's "Under Two Flags" she returned to Mr. Belasco and made her début as a star in December, 1902, as Yo-San in "The Darling of the Gods." The long run which this play enjoyed was followed by an equal success as the Girl in "The Girl of the Golden West." Miss Bates's latest rôle is Anna Granger in "The Fighting Hope."

IN "UNDER TWO FLAGS"

MISS BLANCHE BATES

IN "THE GIRL OF THE GOLDEN WEST"

IN "THE DARLING OF THE GODS"
Photograph by Byron

IN "THE AMBASSADOR"

IN "THE WITCHING HOUR"

Mr. JOHN MASON

IN "THE NEW YORK IDEA"

BY all the influences of heredity, John Mason should have been a musician. He is one of the American family of Masons who have been so conspicuous for generations in the manufacture of musical instruments. His grandfather was Lowell Mason, the great hymnist who wrote "Nearer My God To Thee." His uncle was William Mason, the composer and organist. While a boy he spent five years at school in Germany, and polished off at home during a year at Columbia. His father intended him, not for music, but for law, but a strong natural inclination bent him, not to the law, but to the stage.

He had already appeared occasionally in amateur theatricals when an opportunity was offered to appear professionally and play two servant parts in "The Pride of the Market," which was to be presented at Barnard's Museum, now Daly's Theatre. One week rounded its brief existence, and Mason went to Italy to study singing. After a year abroad he returned and made another beginning in the spring of 1878 in small parts with Maggie Mitchell, and followed rough touring with a season at the Walnut Street Theatre stock company in Philadelphia.

In the summer of 1879 he was admitted to the Boston Museum stock company and played there continuously for seven years except for the season of 1884 and 1885, when he was absent for brief engagements in support of Edwin Booth, Nat Goodwin, and Robert Mantell and, at the Union Square Theatre. The penetration, poise and polish which have made him one of the most genuine and effective players on the stage to-day began to be manifest in the course of the varied training at the Museum.

He disappeared from the company suddenly in 1891, and was heard of next in London with George Alexander, where he played Simeon Strong, the one American character in "The Idler." London liked him and kept him for two years. His return to America began a shifting period of acting. He starred alone in "If I Were You," went again to London to play Colonel Moberly in "Alabama," and returned to star with Marion Manola in a musical version of "Friend Fritz."

When Viola Allen produced "The Christian" at the Knickerbocker in 1898 Mr. Mason was the Horatio Drake, and the list of what he has accomplished since is a list of as fine performances of modern rôles as our stage can boast. He played the leading parts in the American productions of "Wheels Within Wheels," "The Ambassador," "The Interrupted Honeymoon," "The Man of Forty," "Mice and Men," "The Younger Mrs. Parling," "The Altar of Friendship," and with Mrs. Fiske he acted Lovborg in "Hedda Gabler" and created Paul Sylvaine in "Leah Kleschna," Michael Kerouac in "The Light From St. Agnes," and John Karslake in "The New York Idea." Appearances in vaudeville and with Virginia Harned in "Anna Karenina" preceded his performance of Jack Brookfield, the gambler, as a star in Augustus Thomas's play, "The Witching Hour."

IN "THE MESSENGER BOY"
IN "THE REJUVENATION OF AUNT MARY"

MISS MAY ROBSON

THE character actress was one of the well-defined classes in the old stock companies. She has been largely superseded by the invasion of realism on the stage, which has come to demand the type in the flesh rather than in the make-up box. May Robson, however, is a character actress who maintains her prestige because she has the gift to give make-up and characterization the illusion of reality. To rare talents for individualizing a character she adds rare gifts for comedy and burlesque.

Miss Robson was born in the Australian bush. When a young girl she was brought to England and put in a convent at Highgate, and later she studied in Brussels and Paris. At sixteen she ran away from home and married a boy of eighteen, and they sought a home in Texas, near Fort Worth. After several years of hardship, she found herself in New York a widow with three little children to support. She crocheted woolen hoods and designed dinner cards. Two of the children died, the sale of cards declined, and she went on the stage.

Her first appearance was made in "The Hoop of Gold." She played Tilly, a London slavey, and made a hit. But for all that she had to paint dinner cards for two years more. Then she acted Miss Ashforth in "The Private Secretary." Later she became a member of the Lyceum and of the Empire companies. Noteworthy among her many creations are her slavey in "Liberty Hall," Bundy in "Gudgeons," Miss Prism in "The Importance of Being Earnest," Mme. Benoit in "Bohemia," Mrs. Voskins in "Lord and Lady Algy," Miss Yesmama, with her three-legged dance, in "The Poet and the Puppets," and Queen Elizabeth in Paul Kester's "Dorothy Vernon of Haddon Hall." For a short time Miss Robson was one of the fun makers at Weber's Theatre. Since 1907 she has been a star in "The Rejuvenation of Aunt Mary."

MISS GERTRUDE COGHLAN

THE name of Coghlan is one which embalms some of the best traditions of the American theatre during the last third of the nineteenth century. During that period Charles Coghlan flourished as a forceful and polished leading man and as a writer of plays, and Rose Coghlan held a foremost place among the actresses of high comedy and was unequaled in her portrayal of the "Woman at Bay." In 1893 another Coghlan came to the stage to add new traditions to the name in the person of Gertrude, the daughter of Charles, who made her professional début in her father's company in Detroit that year, playing the small part of Mion, in "Diplomacy."

Miss Coghlan was born in London. She studied in the Art School at South Kensington and attained considerable proficiency in drawing and painting. Her first New York appearance was made at the Fifth Avenue Theatre, December 21, 1897, when she acted Juliet in support of her father in his own play, "The Royal Box." Her success was considerable, but instead of remaining in New York she entered upon a series of long tours, generally as a star, playing Celia in "The Royal Box," Becky Sharp in her father's version of Thackeray's "Vanity Fair," as Doña Ana in "Once Upon a Time" and in "The Sword of Justice," "Alice of Old Vincennes," "The Sporting Duchess" and "One of Our Girls."

Once during this time Miss Coghlan was seen in New York when she acted Manuela in Mrs. Patrick Campbell's production of Sardou's "The Sorceress." She took her permanent place as a metropolitan leading woman, however, after she had appeared with much favor in most of the larger cities of the country as Shirley Rossmore in "The Lion and the Mouse." In 1908 she created Beth in "The Traveling Salesman" at the Liberty Theatre and the next season played Lady Proudfoot in Maugham's "The Noble Spaniard" at the Criterion in Robert Edeson's support. Miss Coghlan is the wife of Augustus Pitou, Jr., a son of one of New York's oldest managers.

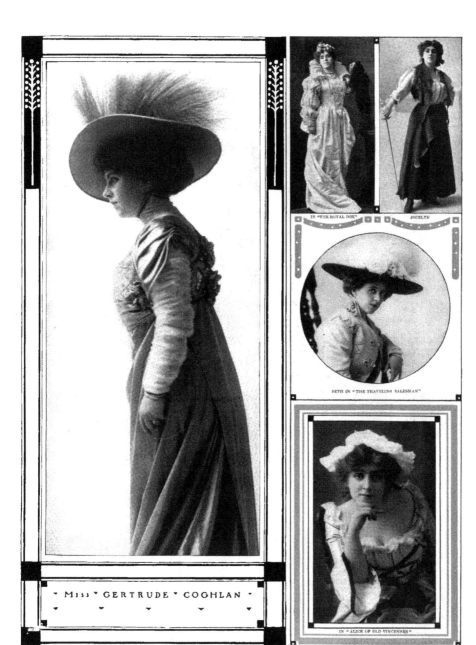

IN "GALLOPS"

IN "THE ROSE OF THE RANCHO"

MR. CHARLES RICHMAN

IN "MISS HOBBS"

IN "THE TWIN SISTERS"

IN "MRS. DANE'S DEFENCE"

CHARLES RICHMAN was born in Chicago in 1870. His first choice of a profession was the law, but while he studied he acted often in amateur theatricals, until finally he succumbed to the call of the theatre.

His first engagements were in small touring companies. This experience lacked monotony in all respects except the promptness with which the companies disbanded. In the spring of 1894 he secured his first part in a metropolitan production, playing with James A. Herne in "Margaret Fleming," at the Fifth Avenue Theatre, New York. From his first appearance he was recognized as a young actor of genuine promise. After creating Gottwald in "Hannele," he crossed to Palmer's Theatre where at various times he played in "Esmeralda," "New Blood," "The New Woman," "The Fatal Card," and in support of Mrs. Langtry in "Gossip."

In 1896 he became leading man at Daly's. With Ada Rehan he played with distinction in the productions of "The Countess Gucki," "The Lady of Ostend," "Madame Sans Gêne," and "The Great Ruby," and revealed further gifts as Orlando in "As You Like It," Benedick in "Much Ado About Nothing," Ferdinand in "The Tempest," Ford in "The Merry Wives of Windsor," Bassanio in "The Merchant of Venice," Charles Surface in "The School for Scandal," and Felix in "The Wonder." He acted with the Daly company in England in 1897.

When Mr. Daly died he went to the old Lyceum, where, with Annie Russell, he acted Wolff Kingsearl in "Miss Hobbs," and Prince Victor in "The Royal Family," two unalloyedly delightful performances. In December, 1900, he became leading man at the Empire Theatre. In this company he acted Sir Daniel Cartaret in "Mrs. Dane's Defense," a distinguished performance; Julian Beauclerc in "Diplomacy," Orlando in "The Twin Sisters," Rev. Walter Maxwell in "The Unforeseen," and Sir Henry Milanor in "The Wilderness."

Since 1903 he has appeared in stock, on tour with Ada Rehan, and as a star in several productions, notably "Captain Barrington," "Gallops" and his own play "The Revellers." The last character he created is in "A Man's World" with Mary Mannering.

Miss Chrystal Herne

MARIE IN "REGENERATION"

IN "THE MELTING POT"

CHRYSTAL HERNE is the daughter of the two earliest exponents of modern realistic drama and of naturalistic stage management in the American theatre, Mr. and Mrs. James A. Herne. Her talents were developed and her skill was augmented by her performances under her father's direction during her first two years on the stage and his last two before his death. She made her debut at sixteen in an insignificant part in Mr. Herne's play, "The Reverend Griffith Davenport," in 1899, and in the first production of "Sag Harbor" she played Jane Caldwell. After her father's death she played the principal rôles in "Sag Harbor" and "Shore Acres."

The first time she acted a part written by any other than her father was in 1903 when she joined E. H. Sothern and played the Queen in "Hamlet" and Huguette in "If I Were King." From this engagement forward she has been a leading woman with Nat Goodwin, Arthur Byron, Arnold Daly, and has played more than fifty characters.

Among her most important and significant performances have been Hippolyta in "A Midsummer-Night's Dream" with N. C. Goodwin; in "Major André" with Arthur Byron; Ruth Clayton in "Home Folks"; Helen Warner in her sister's play, "Richter's Wife"; the title rôle in "Candida," The Lady in "A Man of Destiny," Gloria in "You Never Can Tell," Vivie Warren in "Mrs. Warren's Profession," Nora in "John Bull's Other Island," Raina in "Arms and the Man," and Marie Deering in "Regeneration," a dramatization of Owen Kildare's "My Mamie Rose," with Arnold Daly; Doris Chapin in "The Stepsister," Vera Revendal in Zangwill's "The Melting Pot," and the name part in "Miss Philura."

When an effort was made in 1906 to establish an endowed theatre in Chicago Miss Herne became the leading woman of the company.

IN "THE MAN FROM MEXICO"
Photograph by Byron

IN "THE PATRIOT"

IN "THE MAN FROM MEXICO"
Photograph by Byron

IN the late seventies "H. M. S. Pinafore" enjoyed a vogue which is unique in the history of amusements. In addition to companies of adults there were juvenile companies playing Gilbert and Sullivan's opera in all parts of the country. The fever caught William Collier, in 1879, then in his tenth year, and he ran away from home and joined one of the juvenile companies. He was Arthur Dunn's understudy as Dick Deadeye, for which he received three dollars and fifty cents a week and one dollar and a half extra for handling baggage. Before the season was over the boy had played nearly every part in the opera, including Josephine and Little Buttercup.

Mr. Collier comes from a family of actors, but after his first experience his father kept him off the stage and at school from his eleventh till his fourteenth year. In 1882 he engaged himself to Augustin Daly as call boy at his Theatre. He remained there six years, occasionally playing small parts. As a dude, without a line to speak, in "Samson and Goliath," he proved so amusing that he was engaged as a principal for the clever company which presented "The City Directory." His part was a short one of six lines, but he elaborated it until it became the leading part of the piece. This ability ripened later in several amusing comedies from his own pen.

He continued to act in farces, including several by the late Charles Hoyt, without any significant success until he created Benjamin Fitzhugh in "The Man From Mexico," which advanced him to stardom in the year 1901. His comedies since then have been "Mr. Smooth," "On the Quiet," "The Diplomat," "Miss Philadelphia," "Personal," "Are You My Father?" "A Fool and His Money," "The Dictator," "The Heart of a Sparrow," "Caught in the Rain," "The Patriot," and "A Lucky Star."

Of these pieces he wrote "Mr. Smooth," "Caught in the Rain," "The Patriot," and "Miss Philadelphia." For a while he was a member of the celebrated Weber and Fields organization. In 1905 he played "The Dictator" and "On the Quiet" with success at the Comedy Theatre in London, and the following year he played his most popular parts in Australia.

IN "ZIRA"

IN "THE STRENGTH OF THE WEAK"

MISS FLORENCE ROBERTS

ALTHOUGH Florence Roberts was born in New England and within the past few years has given performances of the first order there, she is less generally known on the Atlantic seaboard than on the Pacific, where she is as highly esteemed as any actresses who come to them across the Rocky Mountains.

Miss Roberts crossed the continent first when a little girl with her cousin, that excellent character actor, Theodore Roberts, and grew up in San Francisco. She acted first at the Baldwin Theatre there, and after two years joined Lewis Morrison's company. He was in the full swing of that score of years during which he packed the theatres night after night in every city on the continent with his famous performance of Mephistopheles in "Faust." Miss Roberts at first played small parts in this play, but soon she was promoted to the rôle of Marguerite, which she acted for nine seasons. During this time Miss Roberts and Mr. Morrison were married. He was a seasoned actor of the old school and his training gave her a solid technical foundation on which her fine intelligence has welded the best that modern methods suggest. In their vain effort to deflect the public interest from the Devil they often gave performances of Shakespearian plays and Miss Roberts acted Juliet, Rosalind, Portia, Katherine and Ophelia.

Her engagement as a stock star at the Alcazar Theatre in San Francisco during the summer of 1898 broke this business association but not the domestic partnership, which continued with a rare devotion on both sides until Mr. Morrison's death. San Francisco made her its idol from that first summer at the Alcazar, and she played long engagements there under her own management every year, supplementing them with extraordinarily profitable tours of the trans-Mississippi States. Miss Roberts secured plays and presented them in San Francisco immediately their favor was established in New York, and in her list are the only American performances of some European successes.

Among the rôles of which she has made herself the favorite interpreter on the Pacific Coast are Sapho, Tess of the D'Urbervilles, Lady Ursula, Marta of the Lowlands, Lady Teazle, La Tosca, Nell Gwynne, Nora, Countess Valeska and Zira. She holds the record for consecutive performances of one play in San Francisco, having acted "Zaza" for twelve weeks. In 1905 she began to exploit new plays and has produced "The Strength of the Weak," "Ann La Mont," "The House of Bondage," "Maria Rosa" from the Spanish, and D'Annunzio's "La Gioconda," of which she has given the only performance in English. She has appeared in New York twice within the past four years. In 1906 she acted in "The Strength of the Weak," at the Liberty, and in 1907 she originated the rôle of Body in Edwin Milton Royle's allegory, "The Struggle Everlasting," at the Hackett. On both occasions she was received with enthusiastic acclaim. During the winter of 1909 and 1910 she toured in a repertoire consisting of "The Movers," "The Transformation" and "Gloria."

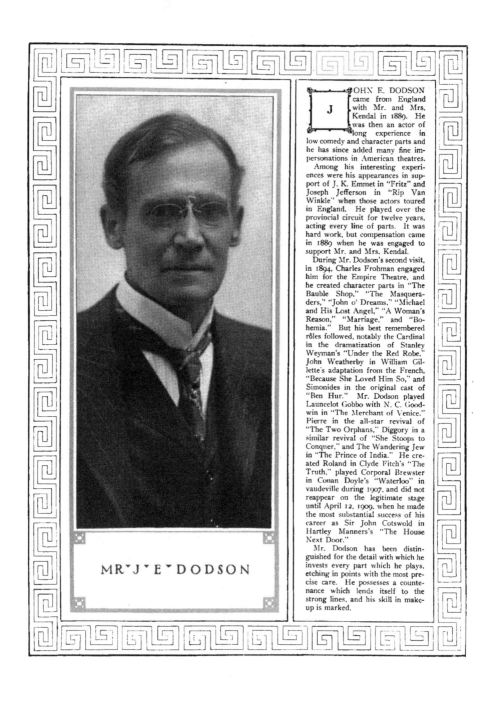

MR·J·E·DODSON

JOHN E. DODSON came from England with Mr. and Mrs. Kendal in 1889. He was then an actor of long experience in low comedy and character parts and he has since added many fine impersonations in American theatres.

Among his interesting experiences were his appearances in support of J. K. Emmet in "Fritz" and Joseph Jefferson in "Rip Van Winkle" when those actors toured in England. He played over the provincial circuit for twelve years, acting every line of parts. It was hard work, but compensation came in 1889 when he was engaged to support Mr. and Mrs. Kendal.

During Mr. Dodson's second visit, in 1894, Charles Frohman engaged him for the Empire Theatre, and he created character parts in "The Bauble Shop," "The Masqueraders," "John o' Dreams," "Michael and His Lost Angel," "A Woman's Reason," "Marriage," and "Bohemia." But his best remembered rôles followed, notably the Cardinal in the dramatization of Stanley Weyman's "Under the Red Robe," John Weatherby in William Gillette's adaptation from the French, "Because She Loved Him So," and Simonides in the original cast of "Ben Hur." Mr. Dodson played Launcelot Gobbo with N. C. Goodwin in "The Merchant of Venice," Pierre in the all-star revival of "The Two Orphans," Diggory in a similar revival of "She Stoops to Conquer," and The Wandering Jew in "The Prince of India." He created Roland in Clyde Fitch's "The Truth," played Corporal Brewster in Conan Doyle's "Waterloo" in vaudeville during 1907, and did not reappear on the legitimate stage until April 12, 1909, when he made the most substantial success of his career as Sir John Cotswold in Hartley Manners's "The House Next Door."

Mr. Dodson has been distinguished for the detail with which he invests every part which he plays, etching in points with the most precise care. He possesses a countenance which lends itself to the strong lines, and his skill in make-up is marked.

MR. J. E. DODSON

SIR JOHN COTSWOLD IN "THE HOUSE NEXT DOOR"

JOHN WEATHERBY IN "BECAUSE SHE LOVED HIM SO"

SIMONIDES IN "BEN HUR"

IN "THE PRINCE OF INDIA"

IN "FLUFFY RUFFLES"

Photograph by Frank C. Bangs

Miss HATTIE WILLIAMS

HATTIE WILLIAMS is a comedienne who has found favor equally by her acting and her singing. For a number of years she has been made conspicuous as a star by Charles Frohman, but this distinction was led up to by a climb which had its pauses on every round of the ladder of her profession.

Miss Williams made her first professional appearance in Boston in the chorus of the musical extravaganza "1492," in which her talents readily attracted attention, and she was promoted almost at once to the part of the Infanta Catalina for the New York run. A. M. Palmer engaged her for the dancing girl in the original production of "Trilby" and then Charles Hoyt gave her a series of parts in his farces.

Up to this time the public had no exact acquaintance with her as an individual player, but she fixed herself definitely in the theatre-goers' memories as a skilful comedienne by her performance of the Girl in "The Girl from Maxim's." Since then she has alternated comedy with and without music. She was one of the lively features of "The Rogers Brothers at Harvard," in 1902, and has since created or been the first American player of the following parts: Vivian Rogers in Leo Ditrichstein's farce, "Vivian's Papas"; Winnie Harborough, "The Girl," in "The Girl from Kay's," Pauline in "Yvette"; and Ilona in "The Rollicking Girl."

When Charles Frohman presented "The Little Cherub" in America he placed Miss Williams at the head of the company as a star in the rôle of Molly Montrose. In 1908 the "Fluffy Ruffles" pictures were given such prominence that it was decided to place that mythical miss in a musical piece. Clyde Fitch wrote the comedy and it became Miss Williams's second part as a star. She omitted music from her next venture, appearing as Athol Forbes in "Detective Sparkes."

MR. ARNOLD DALY

ARNOLD DALY'S distinction up to date is the measure of success he had in producing a number of Bernard Shaw's plays in America. Since the Irish playwright's vogue has declined somewhat from perihelion, Mr. Daly's efforts have been discursive and intermittent. He has not been fortunate in securing good plays, but he maintains his courage, zeal and activity.

He was born in Brooklyn, October 4, 1875. He is the son of Irish parents and was christened Peter Daly. His first engagement in the theatre was as callboy at the old Lyceum Theatre, but his first appearance on the stage was made on tour as a butler in "The Jolly Squire" with Fanny Rice. This was in 1892, and it was after three years "on the road" that he made his New York début in Frank Mayo's "Pudd'nhead Wilson," succeeding Edgar L. Davenport in the rôle of Chambers. This performance at once attracted attention and thereafter Mr. Daly rarely lacked for good engagements or failed to give a good account of himself. Among many parts played he created characters in "Because She Loved Him So," "A Fool and His Money," "The Bird in the Cage," with Julia Marlowe in "Barbara Frietchie," in which he acted the crazy brother, "Hearts Aflame," "Cynthia," and "The Girl From Dixie."

From the time Richard Mansfield had introduced Shaw to America by his productions of "Arms and the Man" in 1894 and "The Devil's Disciple" in 1897, the Irishman's plays had no place on our stage. Arnold Daly became interested in acting several of the other pieces and, surmounting many obstacles, he had the satisfaction of making "Candida" and "You Never Can Tell" popular during runs of considerable duration. He then presented "The Man of Destiny," "How She Lied to Her Husband," "John Bull's Other Island" and "Mrs. Warren's Profession."

After a brief effort to establish a so-called Theatre of Ideas at the Berkeley Lyceum where he produced a number of original and excellent one act pieces, he passed under the management of Liebler and Company, with whose co-operation he has presented Owen Kildare's "Regeneration," which was a dramatization of "My Mamie Rose," "His Wife's Family," McClellan's "The Pickpockets" and a translation of Paul Hervieu's "Know Thyself."

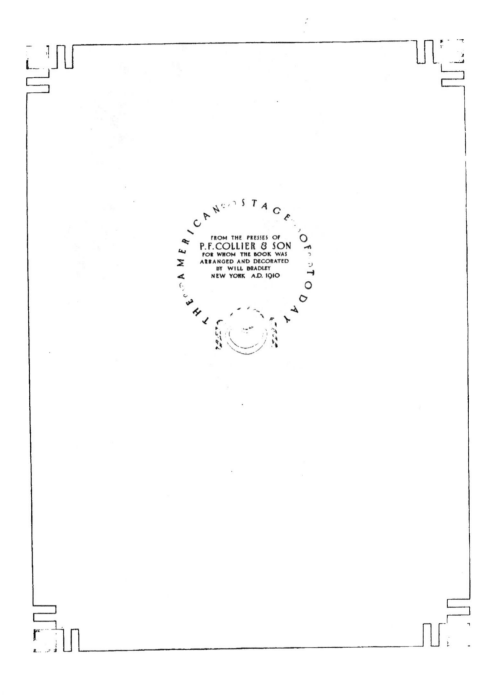

FROM THE PRESSES OF
P. F. COLLIER & SON
FOR WHOM THE BOOK WAS
ARRANGED AND DECORATED
BY WILL BRADLEY
NEW YORK A.D. 1910

THE AMERICAN STAGE OF TO-DAY

CPSIA information can be obtained
at www.ICGtesting.com
Printed in the USA
BVHW042204140221
600083BV00035B/86